CULTURE CLASH

CULTURE CLASH

My Stories of Growing Up
in Puerto Rico and New York City

José A. Camacho

Published by Sharon Camacho, Mount Kisco, NY
© 2023 by Sharon Camacho

Printed in the United States of America

ISBN (paperback): 979-8-218-26189-4
ISBN (ebook): 979-8-218-26190-0

Editor: Jessica Vineyard, Red Letter Editing, www.redletterediting.com.
Cover and interior design by Constellation Book Services

THE PLACE I GO TO BE ALONE

The place where I like to go to be alone is at my seat before my computer, where I can think about what I should write about. If you looked at me from another place in space, you would think I was alone, but if you could inhabit my mind, you would see that many other people—some real, some imagined, some alive, some ghosts—are there with me. But if you did not know me or my experience, these people and scenes would make no sense to you. They would seem like life as a jigsaw puzzle with all the pieces scattered around helter-skelter, or like a dream that jumps from scene to scene without sense or purpose. My job as a writer is to fit these pieces together so they can have meaning to you, as they have for me.

José Camacho, September 2014

Contents

Introduction ... 1

Part I : Growing Up in Caguas

1: The Cowardly Family ... 5
2: A Child's Christmas in Caguas ... 7
3: The Kernel of Corn ... 9
4: Trading Houses ... 11
5: Los Tres Reyes Magos ... 12
6: A Christmas *Lechon* ... 14
7: The Furies ... 16
8: *Huracan* ... 18

Part II: Abuela

9: Abuela's Hen Garden ... 21
10: Tarzan in Abuela's Garden ... 23
11: *Ataques* ... 26

Part III: Abuelo

12: The Lottery ... 29
13: Trading Coins ... 31
14: The Cockfight ... 33
15: Red Pastures ... 36
16: Trading Families ... 38
17: Our Resident Intellectual ... 40

Part IV: A Child in NYC

18: Three Sacred Cows ... 43
19: Trading Climes ... 45

20: Birthday Cake Déjà Vu   47
21: My Family's Nuclear Option   49
22: Trading Schools   51
23: Tigers on a Train   53
24: Immigrant Blues   56
25: The Second Second Grade   59
26: The C Note   61
27: Misu, Misu, Misu   63

Part V: Summers in Caguas

28: Going Back to Caguas   69
29: The Human Telephone   70
30: The King and Queen of Bebop   74
31: The Button Shop   76
32: El Niño   79
33: Don Isa   82
34: Summer Romance   86
35: The Plaza in Caguas   88

Part VI: A Teenager in NYC

36: Parallel Avenues   95
37: Julio Reverbero   98
38: There's No Business Like Show . . .   100
39: Trading Reps   102
40: Trading Work Ethics   105
41: Religious Tourists (to be read in one breath)   108
42: Trading Sexes   110
43: Nilsa   112
44: The Walrus Men   114
45: Papo's Odyssey   117
46: Testing, Testing   121
47: My High School Picture   124

Part VII: Mami

48: The Medium   129

49: Behind the Green Door   132

50: The Séance   134

51: Trading Names   137

52: Trading Faces   139

Part VIII: A Young Man in NYC

53: A Clash Inside and Outside the Ring   145

54: The Devil's Ontological   148

55: Dancing Dog   151

56: A Reverse Baptism   154

57: The Bathtub in the Front Room   156

58: Ricky and the Mad Poet   158

59: Claremont Boys   161

60: Trading Thoughts   163

61: West Side Blues   165

Part IX: A Mature Adult in NYC

62: An Encounter with Eddie of the Second Kind   169

63: Virgil and Horace   172

64: Ghetto and Shtetel   173

65: The Comanche Kid   174

Part X: An Old Man in NYC

66: My Life under the Table   179

67: The Hudson Valley Writers' Center   183

68: The Corridors of Memory   186

69: The Dybbuk   187

70: Trading Worlds   190

Introduction

The author of these stories, José Antonio Camacho, known to his family as Toño, was my husband of more than fifty years. As such, I was privileged to be the audience as he wrote and read them to me. For José, writing them was a labor of love that poured out of his consciousness over many years.

Many Puerto Ricans moved back and forth between New York and Puerto Rico during the 1940s, 1950s and 1960s, a phenomenon termed "circular migration." José documented his experiences growing up in both Puerto Rico and the Bronx in just such a family. His journey, from childhood to teenage years in Puerto Rico and the Bronx, his young adult life in New York City, and into old age, paints a poignant picture of the life of an immigrant who successfully assimilated into the American culture and yet maintained a strong appreciation for and connection to his community.

José was inspired to begin writing these stories after he started working as a caseworker for New York City in a South Bronx location not far from where he had lived as a child. He called this assignment "the accuracy of chance." This return to the Bronx after several years of college and living in Manhattan affected him deeply. He saw faces that resembled those of his people, questioned his connection, and began to call upon the memories of his earlier life, resulting in these stories, written over many years.

Fortunately, José remembered a lot. He preserved in colorful language many of his early childhood, adolescent, and young adult experiences. When he had the opportunity to read them to larger audiences, he captivated them with the emotion he felt and the acting chops that seemed to come naturally to him. He earned and enjoyed the applause he received. While his audiences were being entertained, they were effortlessly learning about a culture at a time and place that no longer exist. I include as well some of his late-life reflections and musings, which provide a sense of closure to his life story.

Unfortunately, José passed away in February 2021 without making a real effort to organize and make these stories available. I feel fortunate to have found Jessica Vineyard, whose kindness, enthusiasm, and skillful, compassionate editing helped make it possible to share these stories with you. I trust you will enjoy reading them as much as José did in writing them.

Sharon Camacho
April 2023

Part 1

GROWING UP IN CAGUAS

1

The Cowardly Family

The first remembrance, when my soul slipped quietly into my body like a foot slips into a shoe, my first conscious recollection is of balancing, precariously and carefully, a cup of steaming black coffee in my trembling wee hands and bringing it to Candida, my aunt, a dark and emaciated figure in a dark, airless room, who, consumed by tuberculosis, was dying a dark and airless death. I was only about four years of age and not yet aware of the risk of this seeming act of kindness, which was met by Candida with a blessing: her joyous smile, which lit up an otherwise drab room.

I, an innocent child, had been selected for this onerous task by my cowardly family, including my grandmother, sister, uncles, and my mother, who had had a falling-out with Candida due to some jealous feud over a since-forgotten man. They were hiding, like a frightened Greek chorus, behind a door, out of reach, they thought, of the tubercular germs that were consuming the dark woman on her death bed.

As a result of this act of kindness, my mother, who was an *espiritista* and was possessed by supra-psychic powers, repeated to me many times that Candida had become my guardian angel, hovering above me like a halo of protective providence. It wasn't, she explained, that I was invulnerable or that Candida was clutching me, like an upside-down Achilles, by my spiritual heel and swinging me above the many pitfalls of this mortal life; no, Candida would just safely guide me through life. However, my mother's words, no matter how well intentioned, only served to frighten me more, for who wants somebody trailing you, whether it be flesh or spirit?

I must admit that in many of my most fraught passages through dark valleys, when I have been most afraid, Candida, or her spirit—or my mother's voice—reassured me of her presence, instilling in me a measure of hope that has boosted my confidence and led me to forgive my cowardly family for crouching behind the door and sending me on a mission of charity that they were too afraid to take on themselves.

2

A Child's Christmas in Caguas

In those days, yes, when the valley of Caguas lay redolent and ripening under the browning sun; in those days, yes, before the shuddering sea pushed the detritus of American products and mores upon our shores; in those days, yes, when the star of Bethlehem still guided the three Magi, *Los Tres Reyes Magos*, through Caguas-Belen to Bethlehem-Belen, and, yes, yes, you could hear the sounds of their camels' hoofs like enameled rain upon the corrugated tin roofs of the village, his mother said, "Toño, to get gifts from *Los Tres Reyes Magos*, you must first go to the field where the redolent valley ripens and collect grass to feed their camels, and water from the trembling faucet to water their mounts, and then Melchor, Gaspar, and Baltazar will repay your kindness with gifts under your bed."

And thus Toño went, together with all of the other young children, still with Hebraic legends scrolling through their heads, joyful, yes, that they could feed the double-pyramided dromedaries of the Magi that the star of Bethlehem would lead, with a golden rein of light, through the *coqui-coqui-coqui*-inflected night.

But to their Hebraic scrolls the older children, whose scrolls were hieroglyphic, murmured, their two-pronged tongues flickering in the electric air, "What hath thine mothers said unto thee? That the Magi, in exchange for your childish gifts, would leave you presents of gold, diamond, and myrrh?"

"Yes, yes, yes," the boys with the Hebraic scrolls replied.

"No, no, no," the boys with the hieroglyphics rejoined, "it is thy mothers who sneak under thy beds with presents and throw away your water and grass."

So that night, no, the boy with the Hebraic scroll feigned sleep to test the power of the hieroglyphics, and, no, as the stars blinked and blinked and blinked with the anxiety of a culture and a land that would morph overnight from Hebraic to hieroglyphics to the most common American denominator, behold, he saw his mother in the fateful exchange.

So that morning, after the blindfold of the night had been lifted from the clear eyes of day, Toño turned his sight to his mother. "Mother, why hast thou lied about Melchor, Gaspar, and Baltazar, when it was thee—the hieroglyphics tongues were right—under the bed last night? I witnessed it with my two unblinking, Coptic eyes."

"Yes, yes," his mother said, "it was me. But I was only the carrier for Melchor, Gaspar, and Baltazar, whose camels' pyramided humps could not enter through the door of our dwelling and so waited outside, tethered by the golden chain, while I made the Magis' gifts exchange. Open, open their presents and you will receive their wonderful gifts."

He opened Melchor's gift: a diamond, faceted with all the phases of his life, from child, to man, to father, to feeder of a thousand multitudes.

Then, Gaspar's gift: it burned with the joys of life, its tribulations and reflections of immortality.

And, finally, Baltazar's gift: the incense of myrrh, with its aroma of music and dance, and love, dangling like a full Carib's moon over the quivering sea, glistening with the moist, electric thrill of a woman's kiss.

And still the enameled hoof-steps tread, and still the illuminated path leads Melchor, Gaspar, and Baltazar and their mounts through the valley of Caguas-Belen to the plains of Belen-Bethlehem-Belen.

3

The Kernel of Corn

Don't quote me on this, but if my memory serves me right, I spontaneously discovered the maxim that the Greek philosopher Lucretius enunciated centuries ago—that nothing can come out of nothing and that everything has a preceding condition—one day in my early youth, when I removed a kernel of corn that had been embedded on a crust of earth adhering to the side of the corroded steel garbage can used to collect the garbage that was kept outdoors in the garden next to the palm tree in abuela's house in Caguas, a kernel that had not yet sprouted the little green umbrellas that some of the other kernels close to it had opened already. I decided to pry open this kernel very carefully with a small kitchen knife, and when it was fully opened into more or less two equal halves, I discovered, much to my amazement and surprise, that there was a little flower in it, like a small embryo ready to open. What amazed me was the thought that things didn't generate spontaneously, but that even the beginning of a plant could be contained wholly within the seed and was not created out of thin air.

This incident was a turning point in my childhood, for it became my first hint that everything has a beginning in something else, and that everything has a history, an antecedent that gave rise to it, so that if you wanted to understand it, it was necessary to study its history. This was, to me, my very first consciousness of history and its process, one that applies to everything that exists, so that if you want to know how we developed as human beings, for instance, you have to look at our evolutionary history. How did the eye develop or acquire its chromatic discernment? It's all there in the fossil record, or better yet, in the DNA, which in itself preserves some of the data that explains the eye, the ear, the heart, the spinal column. Or, as the old professor Casey Stengel would say, "You can look it up [in the DNA]."

Study French, or Spanish, or Italian, or any other of the Romance languages, and behind their vocabulary and syntax is the large shadow of Latin looming over it, and if you go further back, shadows of other Indo-European languages will appear as vestiges in it. The biblical account of the tower of Babel notwithstanding, studies in linguistics can dispel such myths and can lead us to understand how the various human languages developed.

4

Trading Houses

Some of the earlier songs out of Cuba are often about the men who sell foodstuffs and other items from their pushcarts: *el viandero*, the vegetable man, or *el carbonero*, the charcoal man.

Well, *un carbonero* lived in the house next to ours on Vizcarrondo Street, and I quickly became friends with the kid next door, the *carbonero*'s son. Whereas our house was made of wood and cement, theirs was more like a shack, with walls made of newspaper. My friend's room, in particular, had walls made out of the Sunday's comics, and I would oftentimes lie in his bed and read the comics that were my friend's walls.

5

Los Tres Reyes Magos

"Mami," he said, "Miss Betancourt [his second-grade teacher] has selected me to play Melchor in our class pageant of *Los Tres Reyes Magos.*"

"What?!" His mother was shocked, deeply insulted that her son's teacher would select him to represent the Black *magus* from Africa.

It had been so uncomplicated before then. He felt honored that his teacher would select him to play any of the Magi, even one from Africa, but before his mother had brought up the topic, and before her rage, he didn't know who Melchor was or where he came from. All he knew was that he had been selected—a rare experience for someone as outcast as him. Outcast by his classmates because he was, to them, a foreigner, an *americanito*, someone who, having just recently come back to Caguas after a season in New York (*Los Nueva Yores*, they called it), sported American customs. He wore shoes to school, didn't he, and long pants, and wasn't he seen strolling the plaza in a long Xavier Cugat shirt, his face as yet unburnished by the Puerto Rican sun, and his gait, more effeminate *Nueva Yores* than the macho *boricua* strut?

But maybe that was exactly why Miss Betancourt had selected him to be in the pageant, so that the other children would begin to accept him a little more. So that they would not snicker at his *Nueva Yores* outfit, or laugh outright when he inadvertently lapsed into English, like the time when she called on him during the class on how soap is made, when he raised his hand and said he had had that class in the grade before in New York and proceeded to explain the whole process in English while the class roared with laughter.

She had to stop him.

"Toño," she said, "do you know why the whole class is laughing?"

"No, Miss Betancourt," he answered, "I have no idea."

In the playground, he was the slowest and clumsiest runner, shoe-shod while the other boys were barefoot; pant-legged while the others were short-panted.

Bringing him into the pageant was her way of trying to have him assimilate. Therefore, it came as a shock to her when Toño's mother showed up after school, with Toño in tow, demanding, fury-faced, why she, Miss Betancourt, had selected him to play Melchor. Didn't she, Miss Betancourt, know that Melchor was Negro and that he was from Africa? Did Toño look Negro to her? Did he look like he came from Africa?

There was no accommodating the fury face except for a change in the casting, and Toño was now to play Baltazar, which finally pleased and eased his mother. But Miss Betancourt could see the rosy cheeks of embarrassment blooming briefly on Toño's face.

Now that his mother had taken care of the miscasting, she spring-boarded wholeheartedly into wardrobe management, taking Toño directly from the school to her seamstress cousin, Tita, for her to make his Magi gown and crown: the gown, a thing of beauty, silky sky-blue, with inserts of lace for stars surrounded by golden-thread outlines, the crown of phosphorescent gold.

There was glory the day of the pageant—and look! beneath Baltazar's gown, his feet! weren't they bare? and see, his face! wasn't it burnished? and hear his Spanish! wasn't it Rican perfect? and all the children shouted, "*Que vivan Los Tres Reyes Magos, Gaspar, Melchor, y Baltazar.*"

Long live.

6

A Christmas Lechon

It was the night before Christmas, and all through the island, Ricans were celebrating *noche buena*, that good night before the birth of the babe in the manger, about to be born again for the one thousand nine hundred fiftieth time, with songs and dances and feasts.

The *lechon* (roast pork) was being prepared with care by El Colorao, a *peón* who had been in our family since time immemorial. It was El Colorao who had brought the pig that he had roasted on the barbecue spit, slowly turning it over and over during the day, roasting it carefully (while also toasting himself discretely from the bottle of Ron Cañita, rum that he himself had distilled in a homemade still, safely hidden in the *montes* of the Guavate farm). Or, rather, he had dragged and pushed and pulled the recalcitrant animal from the farm to the *matadero* (slaughterhouse), for the animal somehow sensed that, for him, this was to be no *noche buena* but a *noche mala*, and on the way to the house of doom, sensing his bad karma, the pig had resisted all the way, with heart-rending squeals, digging his hoofs into the ground and refusing to move his two-hundred pounds of succulent meat to his personal Gethsemane. It took all his physical strength for El Colorao to move the animal, pulling him by the ears and the rope tied around his neck, and finally, as the last resort, by twisting the pig's tiny tail, his most sensitive area (and which, when cooked, his tastiest part), as a prod to get him moving.

Once the *lechon* had been fully cooked, El Colorao removed it from the spit and carefully cut the meat into smaller pieces, then reassembled it into a whole animal and laid it on a very large silver platter, complete with surrounding trusses and an apple stuffed into his mouth, making him look like a tan and happy pig sunning himself at Luquillo Beach, ready to take a bite out of a luscious apple.

The *morcilla*, the blood sausage, had been carefully prepared by abuela in her coal-fired stove: first, the tripe of the *lechon* was thoroughly cleaned in boiling water and then hung up on the clothesline in the backyard to dry (where, drying and catching the wind, it looked like festive balloons at a child's birthday party). Then, in the kitchen, she cooked the blood that had been drained from the *lechon*, mixed it with rice and savory, aromatic spices, and then stuffed the tripe and formed it into sausages.

The *pasteles* had been carefully made by my mother, with a little help from me. The yucca had been grated on a handheld grater (causing many a scratch on my fingers) and then laid out on banana leaves and stuffed with cooked meat (with many a taste by me as I helped her), then tied and cooked in boiling water.

El Colorao stood as if at attention over his culinary work of art, abuela brought out her *morcilla*, mami her *pasteles*, Ron Cañita flowed with the *coquito* mix, and all through the island the Ricans were stirring with songs and dances in honor of the baby Jesus.

7

The Furies

The day after *Los Tres Reyes Magos*, we went to Mass at the Catholic Church in Caguas, overlooking, and perhaps overseeing, the plaza where budding romances circulated on Saturday nights, like a human-size Lazy Susan for your choosing and delight. Mami, Rosin—the girl from the poor family who my abuela had adopted—and me, in my spanking new khaki soldier's uniform, ironed stiff like a zinc board, and a soldier's cap, sharp as a razor. Rosin and I had a full-blown sibling rivalry going; she could always beat me up in a fight because she was bigger and fiercer than me, and then I would complain to my mami, and she, in turn, who was bigger and fiercer than Rosin, would beat her up, and when Rosin complained to abuela, who was bigger and a lot fiercer than all of us, she, in turn, would beat my mami up, stomping and jumping on her chest like the fat wife with the bandanna on her head in the Li'l Abner comic strip. That, in essence, was the order of the Furies in my household, from me to Rosin to mami to my abuelita.

This Sunday, however, was dedicated to the peaceful babe in the manger. The white-robed priest intoned the Latin Mass and its message of peace and reconciliation, enveloping us in the warmth and comfort of the Nativity. When the service was over, I looked to retrieve my soldier's cap from the pew where I had left it, but it had disappeared.

"Somebody took my cap," I yelled louder than the church bells that were about to clap. That's when Rosin, a snake uncurling from the viper's nest of her heart, pointed toward the white-robed priest exiting the altar.

"You thief!" I yelled to the back of the departing monastic, "You stole my cap, you thieving priest." A roar of disapproval and condemnation rose from the collective throats of the congregants and the bells began to clap, as when the gong goes off announcing the start of a boxing match, and several heavyweight men started to walk menacingly toward us, their fists balled up in pugilistic rage. That was the signal for us to run, to run out of the church, across the plaza, down Vizcarrondo Street, and into the hidden safety of our house. The Furies again took over, with me crying and mami stomping on Rosin for stealing my cap, which fell onto the floor from under her skirt, and the old wife from the Li'l Abner cartoon came out of the kitchen and started stomping on mami's chest as though lungs only existed to be flattened by trampling feet.

8

Huracan

Huracan. Huracan, the word, borrowed from the name of some African deity, always induced in us a certain frisson of fear but also heightened expectations that Mother Nature was getting ready to spank us with wind and rain as she showed us her terrifying power, bending palm trees to the ground and demanding obeisance from them as they bowed down to her like worshippers in an airy church. Preparations had to be made, like stocking up on food and blankets and extra mosquito nets to fight off the fury of the mosquitoes that were driven indoors by the wind and rain and would take revenge on us by trying to suck all the life blood in our veins. And don't forget to stock up on the beer to keep wet our insides while, hopefully, our outsides would remain dry.

Part II

ABUELA

9

Abuela's Hen Garden

My abuela had a hen garden in Puerto Rico that supplied us with fresh eggs every day and chickens—fresh, young, tender chickens—for soups, fricassees, and other delicious dishes that she conjured over a tiled charcoal oven that she lit early in the day, with much puffing and huffing and swirls of smoke that blanketed that part of the house.

These hens—when they were not squatting in the dirt laying their eggs or being chased all over the garden by the raunchy roosters for a quick, sadistic mating, in which the roosters would pinch the tops of the hens' crests in their powerful beaks and, putting their whole weight on them, squash them down onto the ground while injecting them with their semen, after which, while they crowed and rustled their feathers in a vain, male display of sexual superiority, the hens would scamper away in shame and disgust—would spend a good portion of their day digging incessantly in the dirt, looking for worms. Of course, this was an entirely anthropomorphic interpretation from a child's point of view, which is not necessarily poultry's point of view.

What is also an anthropomorphic simile is that those hens, incessantly digging in the dirt, can well serve as a suitable, depressing metaphor for the fact that I am always digging into the humus of my brain for my anxieties, my guilt feelings, my negativities that, like worms in that dirt in that garden in my grandmother's house, are constantly wiggling and squirming in me. I know no rest, which led a good friend of mine, Ishmael, the mad poet, to one day ask me point blank whether I have ever known a moment of happiness.

10

Tarzan in Abuela's Garden

In a dusty old album, Rosin found a picture of me around the age of nine or ten, draped in a faux lionskin bathing suit on a tall but fragile limb of a jobo tree in abuela's garden, the photo I had submitted to the contest of the Denia milk company, hoping to be selected as Tarzan of the Week.

"*Mira, muchacho,*" abuela had cried out, "come down from that tree! You know it's *vidrio*" (meaning that although the jobo tree looked strong, its limbs were fragile, its vitreous branches easily breakable).

But I was almost vitreous myself, so skinny that if the sunlight fell upon me at a certain angle, you could practically visualize my skeletal frame, like you could visualize the veins on the leaves of the jobo tree when the sun shone through it, like a solar X-ray. I was in no danger, therefore, that my light weight would break any of the jobo's branches. Nor did my slight frame prevent me from buffing my self-image into that of a juvenile Tarzan on top of the glassy jobo or of sending that piteous picture of me to Denia, the powdered milk company that sponsored the Tarzan series heard daily in abuela's antique Zenith radio and ran a weekly contest for the best youthful Tarzan. Denia's powdered milk, in those distinctive light-green cans with the image of a dairy cow embossed on them, was distributed gratis in the pediatric clinics in Puerto Rico by the United States colonial administration, and was probably singlehandedly responsible for wiping out malnutrition and tuberculosis among Puerto Rican children.

I didn't win the contest, needless to say, but neither did I receive a nasty letter laced with the sarcastic ridicule that accompanied the taking of the photograph by Rosin, who called me Tarzanitis as she snapped it, for which crack she received a jobo thrown at her that, missing her, prompted the troubled gargle of the hens in the garden as they skittered away from the ricocheting of the misdirected fruit.

Regardless, the image of me as king of the jungle replayed in my head like the repeat of a celluloid film stuck in its groove, making a deeper imprint every time I listened to the Tarzan series that boomed daily from the radio at five o'clock in the afternoon. I kept devising new ways of burnishing my Jungle Jim alter ego. I found an old Bombay-style umbrella that abuelo had thrown away in the garbage, and fashioned from its metallic ribs a bow and arrow, sharpening the arrowheads on the stones in the garden, as Tarzan would have done, until they glistened with deadly points.

I proceeded to stalk the birds of prey that roamed, like wild birds in a savanna, in abuela's jungle garden. I hid among the leafy palm and mango trees for the shot that would initiate me into the warrior caste, until it finally came. A hen, spotted like an eagle, jumped down from its perch on the jobo tree, and as it spread its wings to parachute its landing, I aimed my arrow and shot: the shiny point of the metallic arrow pierced one side of her neck and emerged, gleaming red in the sun, on the other side. The wounded hen thrashed in its agony of death in a whirlwind of feathers and dust.

But the bird's agony was now matched by the agonizing thought that flashed through my mind: that was abuela's favorite laying hen I had just shot! I skipped Tarzan's usual *hahuaa* of victory and the thumping on my skinny chest and hurriedly stuffed the still-quivering bird into a rusty discarded steel drum that had been used for storing water, camouflaging it with whatever dead branches I could find.

Abuela soon began to miss her favorite hen, especially the bounteous eggs she contributed to our morning breakfast. Some days later, with the help of snooty Rosin, she discovered the slain bird in the old drum. Deducing, from the arrow piercing its neck and the stealthy way that the crime had been covered up, who was responsible for the deed, and with her gaze following the index finger with which Rosin—the rat—was pointing at me, she turned red at first, as she was wont to do on such occasions, but then she began to see some humor in it, on a par with my jobo adventure.

"This looks like Tarzan's doing," she chortled, "but at least he could have told me while the meat was fresh so I could have made an *asopao de gallina* or chicken fricassee."

11

Ataques

Abuela's *ataques* did not occur very often, but when they did, it was an earthquake of the body as she thrashed herself around violently in an epileptic-like fit with such fury that even three or four men had trouble containing her.

It wasn't epilepsy that sent her in to such convulsions, however, but the repulsion of having been born a woman, the ignominy of always being subject to the male will with cords that made your actions still.

Part III

ABUELO

12

The Lottery

One lush tropical night, the *bofitero* walked into the house to take abuelo's daily lottery number, his one remaining hope of reclimbing the wheel of fortune, whose spokes the American war had blasted completely. We had been reduced to meals of stale bread smattered with garlic and washed down with sugared water; he was down to his last *peseta*.

Gone was the restaurant business, the *fonda*, which he and abuela had run near *la salida* to San Lorenzo, with its happy customers and metallic singing of the cash register; gone also was the ritual of our helping him count the money at day's end and the occasional quarter he threw our way: two for Rosin, one for me; now the only singing was that of the *coquis*.

He held the *peseta* in his hand and asked me to give him a lucky number, and if I did, and if it won, and if he restored his fortune, he would buy me a pony, a real pony, not that rickety old cloth horse with its entrails foaming out of its belly that I rode in pursuit of imaginary bandits. I stood silently and listened to the beat of the coquis: eight-four-eight. *Eight four eight, eight four eight,* I intoned as I rode away, a Lone Ranger on my Silver.

It was early the next morn; the *coquis* had gone to bed, and Diana's pale visage was a chalky erasure in the sky when the *bofilitero* returned with one hundred twenty-five dollars in silver quarters, which he stacked in neat rows on the kitchen table. Silver and I had to shield our eyes from the glow of so much silver.

Abuelo had abuela immediately iron his white linen suit, which he quickly donned. Grabbing his Panama hat and black Bombay umbrella, he scurried forth out of the house, like a penguin in search of ice, and ice he found. Cool money. He bought a steer, had it slaughtered at the *matadero* at the *salida* to Cayey, rented a *carniceria* at the *salida* to Aguas Buenas, sold the meat, made enough *pesetas* on the first day to buy two steers on the second day, three on the third day, until the first silver quarter that he had played on 8-4-8 had germinated outward to a farm in Guavate, livestock that he raised and slaughtered, and a truck to bring the hogs and cattle to market. He established a vertical enterprise, where all the profits—from the farm to the *carniceria*—flowed to him. Had he started younger, perhaps, and had not the American dog of war so ravaged our tiny island, who knows what it might have been, who knows what it might have become.

I got my pony, though, a palomino named Niño. Niño and I tore through Guavate, not after imaginary bandits, but in hot pursuit of the crazed hens and brainless chickens that dared cross our blazing path.

13

Trading Coins

When abuelo came up the street, visible in his white linen suit that granmami would starch and iron to the stiffness of cardboard, wearing his Panama hat and holding his black Bombay umbrella, Rosin and I knew it was time to scatter.

He didn't want us playing out on the street, not with those *titeres* in the neighborhood, and if he caught us out there, the leather strap would begin to sing its plaintive, painful song upon our skin. So we ran, into the house, behind a tree, or underneath the floor of the house, in the space where the chickens and the spiders hid.

Every Friday, though, to reward our disobedience masked as obedience (the patina children place upon their actions), he would place into our palms *pesetas*, one for me, being the youngest child, and two for Rosin, older and bigger than me, therefore deserving more.

In the floor of the old house in which we lived there was a crack between the floorboards, and Rosin said that it could serve as our piggy bank. The money would drop into that slot and build up until, one day, we would have a silver pyramid of *pesetas* for a bike, a cart, whatever we wanted. So, dutifully, she and I dropped our coins into that crack.

After some time, I decided to creep under the house to view my pyramid of silver but found, alas, nothing but dust and skittish hens. Rosin said she was sorry, but it must have been that the hens had eaten the *pesetas*, an excuse that stretched even the elastic skein of my credulity. Crying, I went to tell mami my story, and she, seizing the situation, seized Rosin by the neck and began to shake her like a maraca at a Cuban dance; Rosin's cries reached granmami's ears, and she came into the room and began the familiar stomp upon mami. Thus did the Furies in my household operate, from generation unto generation, from oldest to youngest, in a ritual embedded in the family lore.

14

The Cockfight

The sun had just shaken itself from its nightly roost and spread its golden wings across the sky when the country folks, the *campesinos*, emerged from the countryside onto the road leading to the *galleria*, the cockfight arena, with their bright rainbow-colored fighting cocks cradled under their arms, and their hopes of a winning session cradled in their breasts.

I had asked my abuelo to let me go with him to the weekly cockfight held, on Sunday mornings in the galleria near the exit to the town of Aguas Buenas, and although it took some convincing before he agreed, there we were, joining the crowd of *campesinos* arrayed in their Sunday best—full white *guayaberas* over wide pants, wide straw *pavas* on their heads—on the way to the fighting pit, abuelo in his stiffly starched white linen suit, yellow Panama hat, and ubiquitous black Bombay umbrella, and me trotting along, like a play doll being dragged along by a careless child.

Abuelo had brought with him his best fighting cock: a reddish English fighting cock, its plumage a crimson rage, its deadly beak a yellow dagger that punctuated with short stabs the still air before it, its spurs sharpened to razor-sharp murderous points. Abuelo was what is known as an amateur cock's man, not in that other sense, but in the sense that he raised a small stable of fighting cocks, which he carefully nurtured and fed on soft bread soaked in milk, and dietary supplements that he and abuela Petra administered in the morning by holding their beaks open and pushing the pills down their gullets with a hen's feather. Under his tutelage, these cocks were trained in the martial art of bird fighting, although, by instinct, they didn't need much training. He equipped them, in the sparring fights with each other, with protective gear, like rubber caps on their beaks and spurs so they wouldn't hurt or kill each other. Their reward, after a sparring session of flying feathers and muted squawks, was to run loose in the garden to have their way with their womenfolk.

I, in my ignorant, child-follows-adult, imitative ways, had tried to become a cockfight arranger myself, in the patio behind our house, where my abuela raised chickens and harvested their eggs. A mini-impresario, of course, albeit a failed one. I had noticed that the black cats my abuela kept around the house were always fighting. In Puerto Rico, dogs and cats are treated as members of the family and have the run of the house; during the day they come and go, usually to eat or sleep, and no one pays too much attention to them. But at night you could hear the blood-curdling snarls of their fights for dominion on the tin fences surrounding our patio. I tried to arrange a fight between one of the cats and one of the roosters, with the unfortunate result that, as I was holding the cat tightly in my hands and making feints with it to the rooster—the way my abuelo would feign a warm-up session between two cocks, one in each hand—the cat twisted its body toward me and scratched me, leaving a long and ugly scar rising red on my arm, a map of super-highways on flesh.

Now I was on my excited way to a real cockfight. The cockfight arena was a round, earthen pit surrounded by a short wooden enclosure, like a ring for miniature bulls, with the owners and managers of the cocks seated around in low-slung wooden benches. Each cock is first paraded around the pit by its owner, who shows to the other owners and bettors his cock's deadly weapons, to the excitement of the betting public and the concomitant engorgement of the fighters' gorges with blood, the bitter presage to the mortal combat. Then the owners let the cocks loose in the pit, and the fight begins: the cocks flay at each other, fencing, feigning, rising up from the floor with their deadly spurs stabbing wildly, their beaks wrecking mayhem until death or flight overcomes their courage, or the losing owner, in order not to lose a valuable bird, enters the ring to shield them.

On that glorious morning of the Puerto Rican *paradiso*, my abuelo's champion rooster was victorious, and abuelo, holding his cock on high, paraded the winning bird around the arena to the wild applause and cheers of the *campesinos* of Caguas.

15

Red Pastures

The house that I lived in as a young child, as a *chico* lad just after the first rays of consciousness struck me like a bolt and I became alive, was on a street in Caguas named after the great Puerto Rican patriot and educator Morel Campos. At that time it was in a semi-rural neighborhood at the outskirts of the pueblo. The house was divided into three apartments facing the street. On the far right side lived a frail old lady, whose feeble steps were soon to be trailing Death down a dark passageway; in the middle lived a policeman, whose puffed-up cherry cheeks, the flowers of heavy beer drinking, disguised a fatal case of tuberculosis; I lived on the far left, with my mami, my uncles, my abuela, and my abuelo, Don Carmen, who owned a large herd of cattle. Once a year he would drive them to our street to be branded by his *peónes*, right in front of the *balcon*, where I would watch in fascination.

The herd, black-and-white-spotted cattle, mooed its way into our street and stretched, like a trembling leather blanket, down to one end—where a blacksmith hammered out horseshoes from crude iron, white and yellow sparks flying like falling stars to the ground—to the other end, where a verdant pasture gave off its emerald fragrance to the street, now filled with the pungent odor of the cattle sweating under a blazing tropical sun. In the middle of the herd, a black bull pawed the ground and snorted with fury, closely monitored by the *peónes*, whose job was to watch that he did not gore the rest of the herd.

Once the branding iron was red hot, some of the *peónes* would wrestle the steer down to the ground, another would tie up his legs, and another would impress the hot iron, the brand of Don Carmen (a C superimposed upon an F, for Francisco, his given name), upon the shank of the beast, with the smoke of singed hair and skin rising along with its moans of pain.

Suddenly, the bull, *o toro negro de pena*, broke loose and charged one of the *peónes*, goring him and pinning him against the wall of the *balcon*, right below where I was standing. It kept thrusting its deadly horns into the man's groin, filling the ground all around, the pavement, the walls of the *balcon*, the sidewalk, with the redness of blood. It overflowed everywhere, like when an inept child fills the page with red crayon beyond the outlines of the drawing, until that black bull of death was tugged away from the gored victim by many men with ropes.

I, the child struck by consciousness, looked upon the scene aghast, and my soul shivered under the little white cotton cloak I wore against the tropical breezes.

16

Trading Families

It was always rumored around the house but never proven that grand-papa had another family. His two sons from that extramarital family were highly successful, one a doctor and the other an architect. But it could have been that this was a self-serving rumor that he himself promulgated in order to make the inevitable and envious comparison with the sons from abuela for whom he had little regard. After all, these other semi-mythical sons were a doctor and an architect; what were his other sons like?

Manuel, who had dropped out of first grade in embarrassment because his hair had begun to fall out due to a mysterious illness, was very smart anyway, and came out with esoteric questions that stumped even the brightest young people around him: "Who is the *el primer ejecutivo* [first executive] of Puerto Rico?" "Who discovered the Pacific?" "What color was Napoleon's horse?"

Lele, who drove a *publico* from the plaza in Caguas and was the chauffeur for a pair of gamblers that he drove to the casinos in San Juan on a daily basis, was so shy and retiring that his speech was mostly a mumble that you had to pay close attention to if you hoped to understand him.

Peyo, who was an excellent mechanic, was also an inveterate gambler who could never hold on to a penny of his money, to the point where abuela, instead of giving him money so that he could feed his babies, had been forced to provide him with milk and other foodstuffs that she obtained from abuelo's farm in Guavate.

And Falingo, who was at the bottom of the totem pole of abuelo's esteem for his progeny because of his sexual orientation, fled to the more liberal shores of Nueva Yores as soon as he was able to scrape the money for his passage on the Marine Tiger. The insinuation, of course, was that none of them could begin to compare with the mythical though illegitimate offspring.

My mami, Chalin, would have none of it, however. She could have been a nurse rather than a housekeeper at a hospital, she would counter, if her Don Carmen (she used his formal title when making this argument) had invested in her education instead of hoarding his money out of misplaced frugality.

She could have been something, she could have been somebody!

17

Our Resident Intellectual

Abuelo was not only the patriarch of the family but also its resident intellectual, being the only one of his generation that "knew of letters." One afternoon, shortly before our exodus to the great Metropolis in the North—where the streets were supposedly paved with gold, and dollar bills supposedly floated down like confetti from the big sky-scrapers in the clouds—Don Carmen was seated on his grand *sillon*, rocking, smoking his Chesterfield, and reading the paper *El Mundo*. On its front page was featured a photo of the steel infrastructure of a skyscraper being built in the great metropolis where the streets were paved with gold.

"Abuelo," I asked, "what is that a picture of?"

"Oh, that," he said, "that is a picture of a house in New York."

"But how do people live in a house like that?

"They swing from the steel girders, like monkeys, heh, heh, heh."

Part IV

A CHILD IN NYC

18

Three Sacred Cows

The Pan American Yankee Clipper rose from the Isla Verde Airport in San Juan toward an azure sky, leaving behind an emerald island gently washed by the white suds of the ocean waves. Soon a sparkling display, the twinkling lights of Nueva Yores, glistened below, diamond necklaces of light that promised a better future for us. The cars below were Sanforized to the size of toy cars, and swerved this way and that, capturing my imagination.

We climbed many flights of stairs to the walk-up of titi Maria's apartment on Fox Street. This was to be our immigrant quarters before we went out to the streets to catch the floating dollar bills that fell down from the sky like confetti. Throughout our climb, I held fiercely to the banister, from time to time looking fearfully down the spiral center to the floors below.

"*Ven aca.* Come give titi Maria a kiss and get my *bendicion* blessing instead of clinging to that wall like an insect," titi Maria demanded. I would have come to titi Maria to ask for the traditional blessing if only I wasn't clinging so tightly to the wall, afraid to take a step forward to the center of the living room. What if the whole floor collapsed, and I and everybody else, all the carpet and furniture, all, was sucked down to the ground below, and we had to swing from the girder beams like monkeys? I clung to the wall like a spider, afraid to move. I had seen black widow spiders cling to the walls of our outhouse in Caguas, but even those spiders eventually have to move, quickly, like a ray of light, when their antennae smell some prey on whom they could pounce and devour. And so I moved, away from the wall and to titi Maria's embrace, very tentatively, step by hesitant step, while the rest of my family laughed, thinking that the altitude on the plane had affected my brain like a spidery web.

"Chalin," titi Maria shouted, addressing mami, "don't you teach these little Puerto Rican boys any manners that they should come to their titi for a *bendicion*? What kind of upbringing do you give them?"

"Tonito," mami said, hurt exasperation in her voice, "go to your titi."

After the mandatory *bendicion*, titi Maria gathered all the men together, including me (as I was considered a "little man") for what she called *una orientacion*, our first lesson in the differences between Old World and New World mores.

"This isn't Puerto Rico," she disclaimed. "Things are done very differently here, *comprende*? There are three sacred cows here: women, children, and dogs. You can't go around beating your woman or abusing her like you might have back home, *comprende*? And you can't hit your children, either, because you can go to jail and your family can be taken away from you, *comprende*? And above all—listen to me carefully—above all, you can't beat your dog and kick it around, because they have special police in green uniforms for that and you certainly will get into *mucho problemas*. Dogs, women, and children, in that order, are untouchables, *comprende*?"

19

Trading Climes

What do you get when you take a nearly naked little boy—a bit of coal burning in the Puerto Rican tropics—and transfer that bit of human ember to cold snows of Nueva Yores? Did you hear that sizzling in the ice? Did you smell that acrid smell of a dying fire?

He knew he could not make it up the hill to his school on 138th Street in the Bronx anymore, not even by pulling himself up on the wire fence on the side of the sidewalk that led up there. In fact, his latest effort ended, for him, in catastrophe: he evacuated on himself. That's what his mother said, "He evacuated on himself," when she helped clean up his mess and bathed him, her flood of questions running with the running water from the faucet tap. In the docket of the bathtub, he finally had to confess under her intense questioning: he could no longer get his left knee to bend. It was stiff, unyielding, a concrete block in the middle of his left leg.

"Your son has rheumatic fever," the doctor at Lincoln Hospital told his mother, "and he has to be admitted for treatment." His mother worried, not only because of his diagnosis but also because in those days, in the early days of the Puerto Rican migration, Lincoln Hospital—a dark, somber fortress of reddish brick that resembled a medieval castle, where the fair maiden is entombed by the wicked *magus*—was known colloquially as *el matadero*, the slaughterhouse. But she didn't have a choice, and he didn't have a choice, either, when the doctor, saying, "This child is morbidly undernourished, and we have to clear out his stomach and intestinal tract, which seem to be blocked," forced a long rubber tube down his nose to suction off whatever material was blocking his stomach. *Phlat phlat* went the sounds of the undigested pieces of bubblegum as they were suctioned out from his stomach and into the transparent globe of glass connected to the other end of the tube. "Aha!" the doctor said. "Now we know why this child is so undernourished and won't eat real food."

In the *matadero* the doctors began to cure his rheumatic fever with antibiotics and to fill his stomach with real food. As he began to walk more normally and his weight increased to a more normal level, the doctors recommended that he be sent to a rehab facility. But his mother wouldn't sign. She feared that the *magus* of the *matadero* was attempting, deviously, to take her son away from her.

So, one snowy, silent night, as the other children in the pediatric ward slept quietly and the on-duty nurse snored peacefully behind her enclosed glass partition, as per a prearranged plan, mother and child crept silently down the stairways of the hospital, out to the street and home, their flight as smooth and silky as the shadows that slid along behind them.

20

Birthday Cake Déjà Vu

It was my sixth run around the sun but the first time I found myself running around a much dimmer sun, having come with—or perhaps better said, dragged by—my family from the hot tropical island of my birth, where I had run around in a tiny cotton cloak that barely hid my behind and was made to put on long trousers and get on a plane to come to the Big Apple, where I could hardly keep my knees from playing a clave beat against each other. To mark the occasion of my sixth marathon around the sun, my mami had taken me to a photographer to have my birthday picture taken.

Like many Puerto Rican children whom parents dress up like adults—because, in their view, children are miniature adults, especially after reaching the age of six, when they are supposed to, in accordance to Catholic teaching, reach the age of consciousness, that is, they magically acquire a conscience of good and evil and are judged accordingly—I wore a pair of light brown trousers and a dark gabardine jacket, festooned with a tie and a Stetson hat. On my face I wore what could have been called a smile, although it was marred by a front stack of ugly black teeth—the result of having been pushed from behind by this nasty tom-girl who lived next door to us in Morel Campo in Caguas, kissing the cement steps from the *balcon* roughly, and knocking out the enamel of my front teeth, which formed a black cave rather than a pearly smile. But mami said not to worry, since these were my baby teeth anyhow, and I would soon shed them for perfectly white ones.

It seems that mami could not get together enough pesos to buy me a real birthday cake, but the photographer said don't worry about it, his camera would supply a cake with gleaming candles. He made me stand, my carbonized smile and all, with a knife raised in mid-air, as though I was about to cut my cake. The camera would supply the cake, but what it couldn't supply was the residue of the icing stuck to the knife that I would have enjoyed licking away in celebration of my birthday photo shoot.

Lo and behold, the camera did its trick, and when the picture came back from the photographer, lo and behold, there I was with a wide, wide smile, wearing my light brown trousers and gabardine suit, festooned with a tie and a Stetson hat, cutting a beautiful chocolate cake with six bright candles glowing on top of it, a cake that I never tasted and I never ate. Oh, did I tell you? My teeth were perfectly pearly white.

21

My Family's Nuclear Option

"No Chinese people live here!" I yelled, slamming the door in the face of the Asiatic-looking man who had come to our apartment on my sixth birthday party; unknown to me then, I was slamming the door in the face of my future stepfather. My mother, her face puffing up with embarrassment like a red balloon, quickly rushed to the door to apologize to her future husband, who now stood in the doorway with his eyes slanting toward incredulity, a hand outstretched with a birthday present for me, like an expiatory offering to a small but angry god.

It was the first of what was to be many encounters between Joe and me, as that original slammed door reverberated in our relationship long past the fading of its crushing sound. Nor was it the first time that I had stood at that door to frustrate my mother in the pursuit of a life beyond the reach of an over-weaned and over-demanding child. As a child of a single mother, without any other object to which I could attach, I clung to her with the intensity of the shipwrecked to a floating log. I would stand at the doorway of our apartment in the South Bronx, blocking her way out for the evening, and despite all entreaties, attempted bribes, offered treats, or proffered threats, I stood determined and steadfast as the rock of Gibraltar, terrified that she would pass through that door and out of my life.

When all these efforts failed to dislodge me from that doorway, my family resorted to the nuclear option: *La Cotita*. *La cotita* was a white, lacy little girl's night dress that was used by some Puerto Rican families as a last resort to bring under control an out-of-control Puerto Rican male child. I was unceremoniously forcibly stuffed into it, as a heretic would be forced to wear an iron mask during the Spanish Inquisition. It was intended to shame and humiliate me into changing my conduct. It was a form of forced transvestism, and I was indeed shamed by it. I would run to hide under a bed or closet at the slightest knock on our door. I was deeply humiliated, chagrined with crimson indignation whenever I caught sight of my fleeting reflection in a mirror or on a shiny surface of a kitchen pot or the glass frame of the apartment door. I kicked, screamed, tried to set myself free, to rip it off, but I could not; the material was too strong and the laces in the back tied too tightly for a would-be Houdini to make his escape.

I finally had to relent by promising not to be the unsolicited doorman of our apartment door anymore so that I could be freed of that suffocating straitjacket. However, inwardly, my strategy was like that of a madman who feigns mental health as a stealth way to be unloosed back onto the world again. I, too, was unloosed to my mad pursuit of my mother's undivided love through whatever doors she fained to pass without me.

22

Trading Schools

The term "circular migration" had not yet been coined by sociologists to describe the behavior of *boricuas* who shuttle back and forth between the Island and the United States—in the case of my family, from Caguas to New York City and back again—like shuttlecocks that go back and forth over the net (the net in this case being the Atlantic Ocean), propelled by the need to migrate to New York to find employment and to return periodically to our homeland, to the warmth of its sun and the even warmer embrace of our families.

Though the term was unbeknown to me at the time, my *familia* was engaged in circular migration, meaning that practically every year, mami would take me back to Puerto Rico and I would be enrolled in the schools down there. I coursed first grade in New York, second grade in PR, third grade in NY, fourth in PR, and so on. I would object, and for good reason, every time Papi Joe would come back from La Agencia Irizarry, the ticket agent where he would buy the *pasajes* on credit for the trip to PR. I did not want to leave my comfort zone by either going there or coming back, losing my friends here, facing the task of making new ones down there, the change in the weather, the language, the climate. But once there for a while, I did not want to come back, for the same or similar reasons. Plus, there was the Superman complex, the dual identity that these yearly changes forced upon my still-developing personality and persona.

In New York, I mingled mostly with smart, sometime smart-alecky, Jewish kids, and fancied myself like one of them: intellectual, worldly, cool. In Puerto Rico, a different ethos operated: in Caguas, shoulder to shoulder with the tough kids from Caguas's ghettos, I quickly had to become tough, street hardened, taciturn, ready to fight for any and whatever reason. Caguas was like the Denmark of Hamlet, where "rightly to be great is not to stir without great argument, but greatly to find quarrel in a straw."

But these changes came about so quickly upon each other that sometimes I was a Puerto Rican in New York and an *americano* in Puerto Rico, with my identity shuttling somewhere back and forth between Idlewild and Isla Verde airports, with my persona left behind in a suitcase at the airport from which I had just departed.

23

Tigers on a Train

Going on the New York City subway was a real trip from the minute you entered the station and dropped a nickel in the fare box. In those days, when the nickel fell into the slot, it was held suspended in a glass bowl that magnified it so that you could see clearly the aristocratic nose on the nickel-head Indian Chief and even the individual braids on his headpiece. Cool! Then you went rattling along, past the art deco stations and screeching curves that you imagined were sharpening the iron wheels of the lumbering behemoth.

We were Marine Tigers in Nuevo Yores (greenhorns in New York), having come over from Puerto Rico on the Merchant Marine ship called the Marine Tiger. And we were a train of relatives who rode the trains in the city: mami, granmami, tios, tias, hermanos, hermanas, bound by blood and by the invisible thread of the fear of getting lost, mugged, or otherwise suffering the untold indignities of the cold and cruel city.

Among the huddled masses of our family riding the subway one night on our way to a family fiesta in the Bronx was Rosin, who, on any given day, was either my cousin, my aunt, or my sister, depending on the changing interpretation of our relationship. This anomalous situation resulted from the fact that Rosin was not a blood relative but had been adopted by my grandmother as a young girl from another family, even poorer than us, in Puerto Rico. Hers was a decidedly Polynesian look, with her flowing jet-black tresses and her shining, black, almond-shaped eyes. Perhaps because of her yet-unsettled status in our family, or her overactive teenage hormones, or both, she was always getting herself or me into some kind of trouble.

One day, a couple of stops away from home, Rosin decided to do a little arm wrestling with the subway's closing door. But the subway door won the first round and held her wrist in the iron grip of its closed position. Struggling mightily, unable to free her hand, and getting scared, she started screaming hysterically, her cries drowning out even the screeches of iron sharpening iron. This brought the conductor onto the scene, who was shouting many choice Anglo-Saxon words and soothing expressions, such as "How dumb can you get?" whose clear meaning even Marine Tigers like us could understand.

This set off my mother, and she and the Klondike bear of a man exchanged more heated pleasantries. "Who are you calling dumb?" mami shouted. "You are dumb!" he yelled back, and "You are really dumb!" It looked for a moment as though they were getting ready to rumble, but before the ring announcer could say, "In this corner, from Caguas, Puerto Rico, weighing seventy-five pounds . . ." the train lurched into a station and the subway door opened, freeing my cousin/sister/aunt.

Out of the subway we ran, afraid that the conductor's resounding whistle would soon bring onto the scene the boys in blue, whose batons could crack any Marine Tiger's head. We ran past the Indian Chief in the golden bowl, whose stoic smile seemed to say, "Don't these poor Marine Tigers have anything better to do than twirl my turnstiles like overhead fans in a Casablanca movie?" Up the subway stairs we ran, into the night of the city that never sleeps.

Once above ground, we discovered that granmami had been forgotten in the ensuing melee, and now, like Flash Gordon in the lair of the Giant Spider, was lost in the underground labyrinth. We rode this train, and we rode that train, looking for granmami, who could neither read nor write nor speak English and who would have been among the lost of the lost.

Finally we found her, sitting on a bench at the Pennsylvania subway station, calmly knitting one of the the famous doilies that adorned all the furniture in our house.

Pennsylvania Station! We were in Pennsylvania! Now we were truly lost. We ran back out of the subway, past the worried Indian Chief, and hailed one of the famous NYC taxicabs. "We're lost, we're lost!" we told the nice taxicab driver. "We would like to return to New York, to the Westside address written here, on the back of this rent receipt." The nice taxicab driver, with a smile and a wink to the meter, whose handle he had just thrown, told us not to worry, he would take us for a ride back to New York.

And take us for a ride he did. Through Central Park, around Central Park, up and down Central Park, until, even being the Marine Tigers we were, it finally dawned on us that we had hopped on an expensive carousel that was going round and round the park, just a few blocks from where we lived. We rushed out of the cab, lighter by a bundle of bucks, and ran back to our home on the West Side.

The Indian in the subway turnstile smiled and resumed his everlasting watch over his underground domain.

24

Immigrant Blues

It took a bit of a struggle for me to get into first grade at P.S. 4 in the South Bronx.

"No way," said the heavyset White woman who sat, like the school's anchor, behind the prow of her principal's desk, "that this tiny tot could be six years of age. No way."

And there was no way that my *mamacita querida*, who had so carefully nourished me in the rudimentaries of 'riting, reading, and 'rithmetic, could explain to that heavy anchor of a woman that her so-called tiny tot was a bit of an anorexic because she didn't know that term, which had not yet become popular in that culture to which she had not yet become fully acculturated.

She would not be entirely comfortable in sharing with an author-itarian figure that the tiny tot, Tonito, had developed the bad habit of refusing to eat most foods, except for maybe once in a while, when he condescended to consume tiny pieces of white bread that he dunked in very light, very sweet *café*, as though he were some teeny bird that dropped from the sky to consume little crumbs of moistened bread. Nor could she share ("share" wasn't a word that she could manipulate in a sentence, nor was it used at that time outside of its literal meaning) the fact that since coming from PR, Tonito complained constantly of being cold, and no amount of bundling him with blankets could make him feel warm, and he would resort to jumping on top of the cover of the radiator and skip and hop from one leg to the other on the tin surface, like one of those blackened minstrels doing a tap dance. It was funny, and the whole family laughed, but it was sad, too, and no one knew what to do to feed him properly, or to keep him warm. Her reticence was not due so much to the short list of English words she carried in her head as it was to the embarrassment of revealing the pain that razored her heart in dealing with Tonito.

So my *mamacita querida* had to yield that first round to that heavyset woman, although, if thoughts could become graphically real, like they did in the bubbles with a point above the heads of superheros in the comic books—which the tiny tot could already read, rudimentarily—you would have seen my *mamacita querida* hurling that heavy anchor of a woman into the Harlem River, which would have snatched her, together with all those gold-gilded diplomas on her walls, into its yawning, churning maw.

So my *mamacita querida* had to write to her *mamacita querida* in PR to please, *por favor*, "get Tonito's birth certificate and send it to me pronto so I can enroll him in elementary school," a process that took several weeks, during which time my *mamacita querida* continued to feed me at the breast of the three R's. And when the birth certificate finally arrived and my *mamacita querida* waved it in the principal's face, the graphic over her head would have been of a red flag that, underneath, concealed a sword by which that bull-headed woman would die, panting heavily, in the ring's blood-soaked arena.

But all's well that starts well, and when I finally kissed my *mamacita querida* goodbye by the school steps and entered that hallow of school life that would encompass my life for years to come, it was with a sense of happiness and anticipation of the joys to come, joys which came sooner than expected.

"Boys and girls," intoned my first-grade teacher, a sleek young woman whose voice tinkled like piano keys around the classroom, "please line up in size places, girls to the right, and boys to the left. We are going to the gym for our first class of the day, which will be square dancing. You are to hold hands while we proceed to the gym."

What a beautiful way to start first grade, made even more beautiful because, lined up with me on the first row, my partner for the square dance was the loveliest *gringuita*, with hair that seemed to have caught the blond sun in her curls and eyes of blue infinite skies, who would have made even Botticelli blush.

My blushes became permanent, like strobe lights washing over my face, and day and night and night and day her image flashed in and out of my mind.

I quite casually found out where she lived one day when I walked by her window, and there she was, quietly looking out. A spot across the street became my daily post, where I could bask in the light cast by the image of the one I loved, silently, steadfastly, but secretly.

O America, what a beautiful country!

25

The Second Second Grade

After the first grade in New York, where I had begun to learn to speak English the old-fashioned way—by singing "This is the way we wash our face, wash our face, wash our face," as the teacher led us in the song and gestured which part of our bodies we were symbolically washing: the face, the hands, the nose, and so on—I went back to Borinquen for second grade to learn how to read and write in Spanish, where I didn't need a song to name the various parts of my body, Spanish being my native language.

The view from the windows of my classroom in the elementary school in Caguas opened up into a green and brown rural vista, where the swaying sugar cane washed like waves of green oceans unto the gentle lap of the brown mountains in the misty distance. That was the view if I looked up; if I looked down, however, to the view under my desk and the desks of other students, I quickly discovered that the other students went barefoot, whereas I wore the fancy, new, grainy leather shoes that mami had bought in New York for me to wear to the new school on my first day of class. When I went out to the playground for recess, I also discovered that the shoes, which kept my feet warm in New York, held me back in the races with the other boys, who flew by me on bare feet without the added weight of fancy shoes.

It was not long, therefore, before the shoes came off, and even though in the beginning the hot ground felt like I was jumping on top of the radiator in the apartment in New York that banged and clanged in the winter, and the thistles underfoot felt like pins sticking into my feet, after a while the soles of my feet grew calloused and tough as leather, and I was able to, if not necessarily win the races, at least keep with the front runners of the class. Of course, mami saved my fine grainy leather shoes for my return run to the icy city.

26

The C Note

My immigrant family, my mother and uncles, all worked for a time in the same restaurant in New York City, albeit doing different jobs, shortly after coming from our famished island to take bites of the Big Apple. My mother—who was probably the brightest of the brood and whom my abuelo held in low disregard—was the cashier; my uncle Manuel, who had dropped out of the first grade in Puerto Rico when his hair fell out for some mysterious reason and was too embarrassed by his bald pate to nourish the brain cells underneath that patina (thus incurring his papa's disapproval); my uncle Lele, who would rather drive a car as chauffeur for the duo of high-stakes gamblers who owned the car and who would call for him early in the Caguas mornings to drive them to the casinos in San Juan instead of his going to school (thus heightening the old patriarch's wrath); and my uncle Peyo, who would rather be under the hood of a car than under the shadow of a book, adding to the old man's anger. They all worked as busboys and dishwashers in the restaurant owned by—can you believe this—a man by the name of Mr. White.

Mr. White, on this particular occasion, had consolidated their individual pay for that week by giving them a one-hundred-dollar bill, the first C note we had ever seen or owned, and which they brought home to our apartment and waved in the air like a flag saluting our newfound wealth. But the salute was but a brief anthem to our game, and we quickly turned to the usual business at hand of Saturday evenings: gambling among ourselves, in which even I, still in the first grade, joined in with mami's blessing and a little stake that she provided, in the hope of improving her chances of winning. The card game, called Monte, was simple: using a deck of Spanish playing cards, two cards were initially displayed face up, and then you placed your money on one similar card to be dealt subsequently from the deck; after these bets were placed, a second set of cards were displayed for a second wager, and then the dealer kept drawing the cards from the deck, one by one, until a card similar to the cards on which the bets had been placed was drawn.

It was a game of pure chance, supposedly, except that one of my uncles, Nacho, seemed to have a much more intimate relationship with chance than the rest of us, and he usually wound up with most of the pot, while Peyo, who had apparently been jilted by the same Lady Luck that favored Nacho, would wind up with his pockets turned inside out. At one point he threw his last *peseta* out the window into the narrow alley below, sputtering curses in Spanish that have no English equivalents, like *cono, carajo, puneta*, but later, when his anger had subsided, he could be seen in the dark alley, like a large rat with a lamplight on its head, scavenging for the coin he had tossed out so he could have another go at the game of Monte.

Nacho had a special game that he played only with me, since I was the "dupiest" one in my family. For this game, he would bet that he could guess the card that he displayed, without seeing it, in front of me, real close to my face, a game which he won all of the time without fail. It only dawned on me years later that, of course, the reason he would win is that he could see the face of the card he was holding in its reflection in my eyes. But among gamblers, the rule is that you never give a sucker an even chance, not even your six-year-old nephew, so I would walk away wiping my tears with the turned-out empty pockets of my pants.

27

Misu, Misu, Misu

On Wednesday evenings, after dinner, we would head out to El Teatro Puerto Rico on 138th Street near Willis Avenue, the entire *familia* moving in synchronicity down the street like a huddled mass of humanity, a one-celled organism with many legs, my mami's svelte and silky legs, my granmami's varicose-veined legs, my cousins' and uncles' and aunts' trousered or bare legs, and my short and skinny legs pumping as hard as I could to keep up with the longer legs, in anticipation of the *Show de las Estrellas* at the *teatro*, featuring stars of the Spanish stage and screen, like the mellifluous crooner Pedro Vargas, or the macho Mexican mariachis like Luis Aguilar and Jorge Negrete, or the sexy Cuban *rumberas* like Maria Antonieta Pons or Tongolele, whose shimmering undulations of gorgeous body flesh would raise the temperature of the thermometer sticks in men's pants to Celsius plus-plus-plus.

But before the *Show de las Estrellas* we would be treated to *La Hora de los Aficionados*, or Amateur Night, when the would-be crooners and dancers and guitarists of (hopefully) future fame would strut their hour upon the stage. If their strut was more fret than strut, the audience would clamor with loud feet and stomping voices, "Trucutu, Trucutu, Trucutu," and Trucutu would come out from behind the curtain with a painted face and Keystone cop outfit, wielding a rubber truncheon in his hand, with which he beat the fretful aficionado over the head and run him or her off the stage.

Victor, like most of the soot-panted, saddle-shoed, Cugat-shirted, pomaded youth fresh from the island, now in New York but still bearing *la mancha del plátano* (plantain stain) of their rural origins, fancied himself, in ascending order: a swell dresser, a Valentino, and a sweet crooner, a nightingale of popular boleros. He was forever singing his favorite song, made popular by Pedro Vargas in one of those steamy Mexican movies that was the rage at that time: "*Hipocrita, sencillamente hipocrita, Perversa, te has burlado de mi,*" which, loosely translated, means "Hypocrite, perverse, you've deceived me."

He sang it over and over, as though by constant rehearsal he could be ready for the amateur hour at the theatre and beat the odds of being pursued and hammered by Trucutu. Partly from having our ears satiated by "Hipocrita" and partly by that mischievous trait in the culture that loves nothing more than to mock and make fun of the pretensions of others, we kept encouraging Victor to perform at the amateur hour. *La familia* warned Victor of the danger of Trucutu, but he was nonplussed and kept swallowing raw eggs, ostensibly to sooth his throat while he tuned up his vocal cords for his hour upon the stage.

We settled in for the show, with all the legs—svelte, skinny, short, varicose—resting from our long walk. Soon enough, Victor appeared on the stage, his promenaded wavy hair and gold teeth reflecting the stage lights beaming on him and on the master of ceremonies, Chevalier, whose witty introduction of Victor sent a shudder of laugher through the theatre. Victor began to sing, but what came out of his throat, constricted perhaps by stage fright, was not the mellifluous tones of Pedro Vargas, but what we call *un gallo*, a frog. *Gallos* and frogs issued from his throat as the audience responded with thunderous cries for Trucutu, who bounced from behind the curtain to mercilessly rain blows upon Victor's resistant head until he was finally forced to exit the stage and then was heard no more.

After the show, the huddled mass of *familia* headed back home, all the legs pumping against the gathering cold. At first we couldn't find Victor. We looked in all the closets, stuffed with our clothes and the myriad garments of all of the relatives we were temporarily hosting in our immigrants' "anchor home," and under all the beds and cots that, like temporary barracks, cluttered our bedrooms. As we looked and joshed (there is no one crueler than a Puerto Rican when it comes to making fun of someone), all the while meowing like cats and chanting "*misu misu misu*" (which is how Puerto Ricans try to coax cats to come out of their hiding place). Finally Victor came out from under a bed, with a red face and embarrassed eyes, crying that Trucutu had not giving him a chance and that the *gallo* and the frogs in his throat would have quickly dissipated.

The next thing we knew, he had taken a plane back to Puerto Rico to let the gentle waves of the Caribbean wash over his disappointment. When we saw him at his birthday party years later, when white caps had invaded the waves of his curly hair and the carats in his teeth were a little less bright, we joked between shots of Bacardi rum about that time gone by, gone by, gone by.

Part V

SUMMERS IN CAGUAS

28

Going Back to Caguas

Going back to Caguas, a town in Puerto Rico nestled in a valley where gentle mountains provide a green frame within which you would be happy to live, would always present me with a sense of nostalgia. Having lived for some time in New York City, there was a past me that I had left here, but I had to step into this old and at the same time new place like a bather at the water's edge, feeling the temperature of the sea a toe at a time.

I would re-meet my old friends, some of whom I hadn't seen for a few years, with joy but also caution: they had changed, I had changed, the world had changed—not with a bang, but maybe it had wandered one degree to the side while I had been away. Although fluent in Spanish, I always needed to learn a different dialect, it seemed to me, and then, as I waded further into the ocean of another culture, its stronger, higher waves made me feel that I should go carefully into that good sea or I could wind up making a serious mistake that could, as they say down there, "compromise you."

29

The Human Telephone

At five o'clock in the afternoon (*a las cinco, a las cinco de la tarde*) the children of the Vizcarrondo neighborhood of Caguas—where I resided temporarily with my grandparents, across the street from Los Tres Brincos, a narrow one-block alley so named, it was said, because in the old days it was marked by three large holes in the middle of the street over which you had to take *tres brincos*, or three jumps, in order to traverse it (but which I always suspected was so named because of the rough trade that took place in that little alley: a little prostitution, a little gambling, at times a fight; if you were just passing by, you were wise to take *tres brincos* and get the hell out of there in three jumps before the dangers of that alley engulfed you)—came to our *balcon* to listen not to Garcia Lorca but to the *Tarzan* series on our radio, the only one in the neighborhood. They would hang out by the cement railing of the balcony buzzing with anticipation, bees buzzing around a hive, and give cheer when the first jungle roars from Johnny Weissmuller and the thumping of his fists on his Olympic swimming champion's chest announced that *el rey de la selva* was going into action.

Some of them I knew from my fourth-grade class at the little elementary school bosomed in the valley of Caguas—with its stucco walls and the green window shutters that opened to a wide view of the gentle, verdant mountains in the background, where the black-and-brown cows with the white spots nestled beyond the sugar cane fields like little figurines in a make-believe toy farm—but only slightly, casually, as befitted a near-stranger like me, returned briefly to his native land after some years living in the "Yoo-knighted-estates" and who, upon my return to Caguas, had earned the title of *el americanito*, a sobriquet I didn't like because, to these Rican kids, anything having to do with America was somehow suspect, second-class, like you considered *huevos del pais* (eggs hatched locally) superior to those imported, as was the same with Rican fruits, vegetables, poultry, even woman flesh, the men stronger and braver who were nurtured and nourished on native soil.

But they came to listen to Tarzan on my radio anyway because Johnny Weissmuller transcended cultural differences and differences in class or status, no matter how slight; as Tarzan swung from branch to jungle branch and rescued Jane or Boy from the jaws and claws of roaring lions and let out his call of victory, the differences that seemed to separate us—they who lived in nearby hovels, I who lived in a cement house and owned a radio and went to school wearing long pants and leather shoes as opposed to their bare feet and short khaki pants and shirts—were drowned out by Tarzan's roars.

Tarzan provided a nexus between us. We would go every Wednesday afternoon to watch Tarzan movies at the Turabo movie house, which, as one of the three movie houses in Caguas, was the cheapest in admission prices and catered to the raucous taste of the gang that hung around our *balcon*. El Alcazar was the most luxurious of the three, with plush cushioned seats and air conditioning, and the one favored by the *flanes*, the more affluent kids from the better neighborhoods ("*flanes*" because flan was a rich dessert that was light and delicate, like those kids themselves). The third, the Arcelay, was middle-of-the-road, and you mostly saw families going there to watch Mexican films. It was a rigid cinematic culture that you ignored at your own peril, like the one time that I went to El Turabo, and when I went to claim my prize for guessing which engine would win the locomotive race featured on the screen, I was pounded by *cocotazos* ("nuggies") freely administered to my head by the groundlings up front so that I decided to forgo my prize, to the vast amusement of the rabble.

But if I was different from them, I was soon to discover that I was by no means unique in this respect, as another student, a girl with lustrous red hair, hazel eyes, and a delicate porcelain face, who entered our class in mid-term (as was soon communicated to me by the gang that hung around my balcony on Tarzan afternoons) was also an *americanita*, a Rican also transplanted from Nueva Yores. Her sobriquet, pinned on them by the Rican kids (it was their habit to re-baptize anyone who was different from them with nicknames that usually emphasized those differences: if you limped, you were El Cojo, if you were missing an eye, you were El Tuerto) was La Pelirroja on account of her flaming red hair.

When I first saw La Pelirroja, I was struck by the beauty of her hair, her skin, her eyes (so different from the Taino looks of the other girls around us, with their sultry dark looks and their inviting and seductive smiles) so that her image went immediately like a nail hammered into my heart. At the same time, though, sitting alone at her desk, with her eyes down studying her book, the veil of fear that inevitably interposes itself between one and the desired object enveloped me, and I left the classroom in confused elation.

However, the campaign between our two hearts was soon taken up by the Tarzan troupe that gathered itself in the afternoon by my *balcon*. Like a human telephone, they began ferrying messages from her to me and me to her. Did I like her? they wanted to know from me, and did she like me? they wanted to know from her. Our answers were swiftly conveyed back and forth by the barefoot multitude, and whole scenes of romantic dramas telephoned back and forth: Did I want to take her out for a walk, a movie, to get an *helado*? Could we meet at the plaza? Could we walk together to school? What was my favorite movie, comic book, song? The human telephone took on a life of its own, proposed its own questions, suggested possible answers, and camps of opinions formed and debated the right strategy, the right approach.

At some point, though, static developed on the line. In the fourth grade, I was not yet ready to cope with the emotions that La Pelirroja had set off in me. For one thing, I didn't have any *chavitos* to take her to the movies or even buy her an *helado*. For another, the fabric of the heart was not yet of sufficient weave to clothe my nascent emotions. So, I took the cowardly way out: to hide my immaturity, I struck a pose of indifference; I became *vanidoso*, and my *vanidad* was readily transmitted to the receiver at the other end by the human telephone. Soon the line went dead; La Pelirroja had hung up on me. The human telephone was disconnected, and we went back to Tarzan, back to arguing over who was the best Tarzan ever: Johnny Weissmuller, Lex Barker, Buster Crabbe? Aauuiiiooaaa!

30

The King and Queen of Bebop

Caguas, in my pre-teen years, was a step or two behind the fashion of the times, and while Americans on the mainland were doing the jitterbug and deepening the décolleté to eye-popping depths, Caguenos were still doing the Vals, a version of the waltz. It was rumored that a woman who wore a backless dress to the plaza on a Saturday evening—when we all dressed up in our finest clothes and went for a stroll in the plaza to meet with friends and flirt with the opposite sex—would be showered with stones, not with deadly intent but just enough to send her back to the closet to redress herself and to redress the public's sense of outrage.

But when Rosin, my step-aunt whom my grandmother had adopted as a young girl from a poor family (in a process well honed by Puerto Rican families, who grew not only by natural births but also by accretion of members who were either adopted or just naturally attached themselves to a particular family), and who, at the time, was in the overcharged hormonal stage of her teenage years, and I, in some nebulous puberty stage, landed back in Caguas after an immersion of a few years in New York City, we landed with a splash, like space travelers returning to earth after a sojourn of light years away and carrying under their arms the specimens of an advanced civilization. In our case, it was the latest New York fashions; me in my *tubitan* pants, saddle stitches running down the sides, severely narrowed at the cuffs; Xavier Cugat shirts, and two-toned shoes, and she in a strapless dress, brightly colored pumps, and glowing accessories, and together portaging with us a Victrola record player and the latest Bing Crosby and jitterbug 45 rpm vinyl records, which we played and danced to in the wild and crazy way that New Yorkers dance, leading our fellow adolescents in Caguas to swing with the new rhythms we were introducing to them. Thus we became, in our social circle of cousins and friends, *muy popular*, were invited to all their parties, and became the king and queen of bebop.

31

The Button Shop

The first time I saw her, when she passed by me in front of my grand-father's *carniceria*—where my uncle Manuel handled the meat sales and I doled out small rolls of chewing tobacco for a penny each to the customers as a little sideline to put some change into my teenage pocket—with her pert walk, her ivory smile, the cinnamon-colored skin that Ricans call *piel canela* (a blend of African and Taino blood so unique to the island and so delectable that its very reference to cinnamon brings that taste to your mouth), and long, black, flowing tresses that trailed behind the most eloquently synchronized buttocks like bongos playing inside of your chest, and when she smiled at me in that coquettish way Rican girls do, it was like, in her wake, the oxygen was sucked out of the air, and my heart was left pumping hard but struggling for breath.

"Aha!" was my uncle's reaction, "I see that you have seen Serafina." Not only I, but also the all the drivers of the *publicos*, whose cars lined the side opposite abuelo's butcher shop at the exit to Aguas Buenas. All the male heads turned, like a mass poltergeist, toward the obscure object of desire. "She works a few stores from here, in that buttons and threads shop down there."

It took a few days before I dared venture in the direction of the street that had had all the air sucked out of it, toward that shop of buttons and threads that I knew enclosed the Afro-Taino beauty who had given me a jolt from an invisible defibrillator.

When I finally did pass by, she called me using my first name, and with her index finger, drew me in with what seemed an invisible filament of thread. How did she know my name? My uncle had told her, and he had also told her that having come from Nueva Yores, I spoke English very well. She wanted to know if I had some time to tutor her younger sister in the subject, which was required in the Rican schools. She spoke to me in simple, friendly terms, like we were old acquaintances casually meeting again, but the full content of her speech eluded me, as I stood transfixed by the melodic sounds that tinkled from lips full with petals of roses.

So, I got rooked into tutoring Amparito, and hooked into spending lazy afternoons in the buttons and threads shop with Serafina, and flirting with her, and flirting with the health of my heart, which went underground so that I could never mine the word "love," that rich ore that I could never bring up to the surface. Thus, she became my unspoken girlfriend, and I her unspoken boyfriend, but it was thrilling to skate around that coronary circle that enwrapped us, to not mouth the words that, when said, would draw a curtain on an act that we were just beginning to rehearse off-stage. Amparito thus became a nexus between us, a connection wherein our desires played a game of charades, the emotions always alive, living subcutaneously, below the surface, never spoken, never acted out except in gestures, looks, sighs.

From time to time, when I could unzip myself from her, I would make deliveries on a bike for my uncle. Once, as I was rounding the plaza for a delivery, the bike being powerfully powered by my haste to get back to the shop of buttons and threads, I took a curve too fast, almost running over two urchins, *titeres*, little thugs from some slum in Caguas—either Savarona, where there was no duke, or El Verde, where there was no green, or El Millon, where no millionaires lived, only ragged men in haggled hovels of poverty. To our unexpected encounter they had brought razor blades, and as I tried to flee, they began to throw them at me, sunlit razor disks twirling through the air. I felt an instant sting in my left earlobe, and warm blood trickling from it. When I got back, Serafina administered first aid to me: physical first aid at first, and then a warm, embracing second aid to stitch up and heal the unraveled threads of my day.

But the seamless garment of our time together would not last, and tears soon began to show.

As though mirroring that child's game we used to play (where two ponies, one black, one white, follow one another on magnetic hoofs on opposite sides of a board), so our parents of different races jockeyed against each other on the opposite sides of the color board. My grandmother began to talk about how "our Tonito likes *la carne de guinea*," meaning by that the dark meat of pheasants, and my mother about how Serafina was much older than me (actually, only by the elastic stretch of a few years), while her father had some residual resentment against my grandfather for something that happened between them, probably a business quarrel in the past sometime. The final, irreparable rip of the garment occurred when my mother treated Serafina with cold, needle-sharp haughtiness the one time when I naively invited her to the house. When she left, hurt and angry, I knew then that not all the thread in this world or in the world to come could ever sew our rent relationship back together again.

32

El Niño

It was after I had given abuelo the winning number for the *loteria* and he had rebuilt his lost fortune (lost due to the ravages that the war had extracted on Puerto Rico) that he had bought a farm in Guavate, located halfway between Caguas and Cayey, a little past that point in the highway called *la curva del colmo*. Its name was a testament to the sharp curve in the highway overlooking a high precipice and dotted with little white cement crosses as letters of stone of a final farewell to the many dozens of drivers who had lost their lives in the unsuccessful managing of the curve. Some of the crosses were for the drivers of the overloaded sugar cane tractors that had attempted the curve like creeping centipedes, and had gone down when the tail of the tractor had been too heavy to make the curve; some were for those who had unwarily come upon these tractors that, taking up both sides of the road, had forced them to swerve and plunge into the paradise-like valley below and, hopefully, into paradise above.

Fortunately for me, riding with my grandfather and his majordomo, Don Isa, and the driver, Tito—whom my grandfather had recently hired and who was only a few years older than me, although he had already crossed that hormonal boundary that separates the boys from the men while I was still only on the cusp of it—*la curva del colmo* marked only a breath-stopping moment on our way to Guavate on that Saturday, the usual day when my grandfather, with a money bag bulging with *pesetas*, went to the farm to pay his *peónes*.

At the Guavate farm, after we had climbed down from the truck and rode the rest of the way in by horseback and mule, Don Isa gathered all the men in the *bohio* of the straw-thatched house that served as the quarters for the caretakers of the farm. Lining them up, Don Isa would call out the names of the individual *peónes* and detail the days and hours that they had worked so that abuelo could dole out their due wages. Abuelo, though, who was so attached to his money that the *pesetas* seemed welded to his hand, would challenge every one of Don Isa's calculations, claiming that a cow had impaled herself on the barbed wire fence as a result of *fulano*'s negligence, or that *sutano* was not yet old enough to receive a full man's wage, whereupon Don Isa would come to their defense, and an argument would ensue between them, the *peónes* standing by silently until some kind of compromise would be reached, usually in abuelo's favor.

Soon, though, I was in the saddle on El Niño, the outsize pony that was my prize for having given the *loteria*'s winning number to abuelo, riding with a tail of dusty smoke behind me, when I came upon Tito, sitting on the fender of the pickup, smoking a cigarette. "Hey, Tito," I called out to him, with braggadocio in my voice that I was soon to regret, "do you want to have a race?"

The race was down to the river, swollen with this season's rain, and I figured that I could easily outpace the heavy pickup truck, which had to slowly scamper crab-like over the many rocks on the road. What I had not figured on was that that *hijo de la gran puta* driver (translated loosely as that son of a grand whore) would come full blast behind me, the devil may care about the rocks, blowing his horn full blast, which sent Niño into a frenzied panic, his eyes dilated to their fullest and nostrils flaring like open steam pipes, galloping at breakneck speed down the dangerous road. *Ay dios mio, he's going to trip and we are both going to die*, I thought as I looked back and waved to Tito to stop. But he just kept on coming, blowing his demented horn and with an idiot's smirk pasted on the windshield of the truck, gaining on us rapidly.

Finally, thank god, we got to the river. Niño plunged headlong into the waters of the swollen stream that, in its wet, welcoming embrace, cooled our panic and enveloped us in a liquid kiss. Niño, with me on the saddle, swam and scampered swiftly to his feet on the other side of the river, where I jumped from the dripping mount and began to scream at Tito, bent over with laughter across the river from us, and threatened to report his actions to abuelo. But after a while, after he had helped me hoist the soaked saddle and cloth into the back of the pickup truck so it could dry beneath the blow-dryer rays of the Guavate sun, we began to see the humor in the whole episode. We sang together, "Dash, dash, dash, we were having a splash" on our way home to Caguas, around the bend dotted with the little white crosses, those little stepping stones to heaven, with abuelo and Don Isa looking at us like we had become unhinged.

33

Don Isa

When Don Isa, my grandfather's *mayordomo* and *toto factotum*, went to apply for Social Security benefits at the Caguas branch, the one near the plaza by the *salida* to Aguas Buenas, the agent there asked him, "How long have you worked for Don Carmen?"

"All my life, practically, since we were teens."

"And, how many days per week did you work for him?"

"Oh, six and half, with the half day being Sundays."

"Well, Don Isa, according to our calculations, based on the time you worked for him without overtime compensation for time and a half for Saturdays and two times for Sundays, it would seem that he owes you . . . x amount."

When Don Isa repeated this story to my abuelo, Don Carmen, including the amount that the agent at the *salida* to Aguas Buenas had quoted, Don Carmen, always reluctant to part with his hard-earned money and nimble in thinking of strategies to defend it, responded in wide-eyed amazement, "Well, Don Isa, I am afraid that I have no way of paying you the money that I supposedly owe you, short of trading places with you. If you really want that money, from now on you be the *patron* and I'll be your *mayordomo*."

Horrified, as my grandfather knew he would be, by the idea of trading places, of turning a lifetime arrangement upside down with a single, solitary twist, Don Isa quickly dropped the demand for the x amount and blamed the agent at the *salidas* to Aguas Buenas for the whole thing, and how could Don Carmen ever think that he, Don Isa, could ever make that kind of demand on him? and let's just forget about the whole thing, why don't we?

So, things stood status quo. Don Isa continued to be my grandfather's *mayordomo* and his best friend, an arrangement that went back to their teenage years, although I don't know if it went back all the way to *los tiempos de España*, which, in the language of the old folks, was way back indeed, like going back to prehistoric times. (Time, for them, was reckoned either by *los tiempos de España* or by the various natural cataclysms that had befallen the island of Puerto Rico, so that they would say, "And that happened in the year of San Felipe," a hurricane that had taken place long ago, or of "San Isidro," a cyclone embedded in the archaic memory of the pre-literate *jibaro* people.)

I still had Don Isa as the major domo, then, and to my haughty *criollo* mind, he was like my personal attendant whom I could order around, but I could only get away with that when my grandfather was around. On those occasions when I accompanied my grandfather and Don Isa to the farm in Guavate on Saturdays, when the weather was nice (and the weather was always nice in Caguas, but it always rained in the afternoon in Guavate, and when you looked from the balcony of our house on Vizcarrondo Street toward Guavate, which was like a tropical rain forest, you could see a cumulus cloud the size of an atomic mushroom cloud always hung over the area), I would say to Don Isa, "Saddle me a horse." If abuelo was around, there would be no problem. Don Isa would tell one of the *peónes* to go fetch me El Niño, the horse that abuelo had brought me and named after me (a joke because that horse was no *niño* in size and strength but was so big I had to climb the *balcon* and get on him from there while Don Isa held him steady; before that, Don Isa would go into the thatched-roofed house that served as the home of the always-changing sharecropping family that worked the farm for abuelo), he would come out with my saddle in hand, the saddle abuelo and I went together to buy in the leather shop at the *salida* at San Lorenzo, the shop with the aroma of leather and leather furnishings like wood polish that was so intoxicating.

But when abuelo wasn't around, Don Isa would say, "Saddle him yourself. I am too busy running this farm for your miserly grandfather." That meant that not only would I have to saddle El Niño myself but that I would also have to look for and find him (he sometimes hid in a very rough bamboo grove where there were hives of bees hovering in halos of anger over his head and that of his brother, Troto, so named because of his shambling gait that resembled a broken trot that made it difficult to ride him). I then would have to corral him in that buzzing grove—he never came willingly—and lasso him with a rough, prickly rope that Don Isa would give me for that purpose.

(At least he showed me how to lasso a horse, how to tie the rope around his head so that I could more or less ride and control him without the need of a bridle; I say more or less because that horse was very strong, of a nasty temperament, and did not appreciate my riding him; even when Don Isa saddled him, the horse would take a humongous breath, fill his lungs up with air, and expand his diaphragm so that in order to cinch the belt of the saddle tightly around him, Don Isa had to kick him in the belly very hard to force the air out of his lungs so the saddle fit snugly and not jiggle all around with me on it.)

Even when I rode him bridled, if he should hear the whinny of a mare far into *el monte*, he would take off, and no amount of my pulling on those reins would make him desist from his headlong dash. I had to wait till he ran out of strength or realized his date for that afternoon was not going to materialize. But I knew that no amount of running like a crazed pony would keep him from returning back to the house at around five o'clock; the pull of the aroma from the oats laid out in the trough for the horses exceeded, in his mind, the fragrance of unattainable love.

I would crouch down very low on his back, holding on for dear life while he took me on his trip around the countryside. Once, on one of his escapades, his ears pricked up, eyes dilated, and he started a headlong dash toward a lemon tree with low overhanging branches; I sensed danger from his demeanor and his accelerating speed, knowing, from the way the tree loomed ever larger in front of me, that this crazy pony had finally figured out a way to knock me off his back and keep me off permanently: by bending his head while passing underneath the branch and having it bat me off his back.

This time I lay flat along his body, and as we passed underneath the branches, I just about nearly made it—except, that, as we passed under, I felt the sting of the branch as it scraped my back. The rest of that afternoon I felt a stinging and itching in my dorsal spine. I learned later, much to the amusement of Don Isa and the rest of the ragged posse of *peónes* that welcomed the prodigal grandson on horseback back to the homestead, that not only had the lemon branch scraped my back but that it had deposited on it a white *plumilla*, a parasitic insect shaped like a white feather. It had mistaken me for a lemon and attached itself to my spine the way it does to the lemon to suck the juice out with its long mandible.

"Ah, here it is," shouted Don Isa as he plucked the *plumilla* from my back and waved it in the air, a trophy of the day's small victory.

34

Summer Romance

There she stood, in the corner of Los Tres Brincos, across the street from where I had been hanging out in the *balcon* of my grandmother's house in Caguas, in a bright yellow dress that contrasted with the cinnamon color of her skin, like a sunflower that had somehow sprouted from the hard cement of the sidewalk, with an expression both wistful and expectant, like she was waiting for someone. That someone that she was waiting for, I was later to find out, was me. I could not keep my eyes off her; I longed to taste the cinnamon of her skin, to run with my lips over those pearly teeth, like fingers running over a warm keyboard, and that lithe brown body that nestled in the palm of my eyes like chocolate for the heart.

It turned out that Gladys was related to me, as she was the cousin of my uncle Manuel's wife, so it was not too long thereafter that our romance ensued and that I would be spending most of the evening hours of my summer school vacation from New York in Caguas, where mami usually took us for the summer, like many Ricans did, to spend time with the family in *la isla del encanto*, the enchanted isle of Puerto Rico. For me, that summer was indeed enchanted, enchanted by Gladys, by her winsome, flirtatious ways, the soft petals of her lips in embracing kisses, her melodious voice that sang love songs to me beneath the canopy of the gentle night, with the cool, complicit smile of the tropical moon.

One afternoon, in the *campo* of the farm that abuelo had acquired after he rebuilt his downtrodden fortune after the war, Gladys and I rode together astride my horse, El Niño (which my grandfather had bought especially for me as a reward for giving him the winning number of the lottery in Puerto Rico), and she perched on my lap as we cantered along, with the strain of our combined weight on El Niño no greater than the strain that her soft buttocks put on my aroused member.

Somewhere in a secluded island on the farm, close to two flowing streams that El Niño splashed happily through, we found a strawberry bush with bursting, ripening fruit, where we settled underneath the brambled branches of the bush in an occluded and secluded spot, and made out, lips turned ruby by the passionate kisses and strawberries that we smashed lips to flaming lips.

As summer flowers and summer romances are to the summer sweet, and fall follows summer as night follows day, both fall and night followed our brief romance when I found out from her mother that Gladys was seeing someone else, an older guy, into whose house a few streets down her mother had secretly watched her enter one night and emerge hours later. The cord of our attachment was abruptly snapped, and I reflected in the sudden dejection I felt afterward that perhaps our chaste romance (I had not been intimate Gladys because of my religious scruples, as I was then in the Jehovah's Witnesses, who forbade fornication) had driven her into the arms of another man with no such scruples. Thus, the bright flower of our romance faded into the vanished background of love lost. Old girlfriends never die; they just fade away.

35

The Plaza in Caguas

Every pueblo in Puerto Rico, no matter how small or poor, had to have a plaza, which functioned as the central meeting and strolling space for its population, and every town or village vied with each other to be able to boast that its plaza was the best and most beautiful one.

Caguas, where I had been deposited by my mother while she worked out her relationship with her new husband, my stepfather, Joe, was no exception to this rule. It boasted an ample plaza, ringed by artfully sculpted trees that were trimmed into shapes of rounded canopies, or majestic pyramids, or fantasy geometric forms, providing the coolness of their shade to those resting on the marble benches encircling the plaza, while the riotous colors and heady perfume of the tropical flowers that worshipped at the feet of these majestic trees added a sense of wellness to whomever lingered under their branches.

Not to be outdone by the plazas of the other pueblos, which had no trouble nurturing trees and flowers that seemed to explode like magic from the fertile tropical soil of the island, Caguas built and maintained a spacious aviary in which tropical birds flew and sang, their vivid colors reflecting, like an upside-down mirror, the magic colors of the floor below. And where else but the plaza in Caguas had an aquarium? Its sole inhabitants were two giant crocodiles in a perpetual state of green comatose, in a pond enclosed by a wire fence on which our teenage crowd would bang and shake wildly, daring them to come out of their lethargy but secretly hoping they would remain still as fallen logs in their dirty pond.

In the cool Caguas evenings, my grandfather, my mother's father, would sit with his elderly friends, all starched up in a white linen suit that was so stiff it could probably hold him straight up in his marble seat, even if his head should bobble and nod down with the weight of many years of troubled sleep as he chatted or reminisced with his friends about won or lost conquests—names that could now be revealed, as some of them were by now public script in the cemetery just outside of town.

Across from the plaza rose the sumptuous steeple of the Catholic Church. One Easter, on Holy Friday, I got the unholy idea of clambering up one of those beautiful sculpted trees, above the impenetrable crowd that had blocked me, to get a better view of the Easter procession, where the icon of Christ was being carried in what looked like a coffin with a glass top. I was practically right on top of it, and the image so burned itself into my brain that I could almost hear my heart sizzling, and the shock of it almost knocked me off the sculpted tree. I doubt very much that, had I fallen, my dead and broken body would have been carried in that procession like a local boy saint martyred by the image of Christ.

Across the street from the plaza was one of our favorite places, an ice cream shoppe that featured the most delicious ice creams, with flavors like mango, coconut, *guanabana* and, of course, vanilla and chocolate—distinctive, cool flavors that would have sent Daisy Borden back to the barn to re-milk her cows. Right next to it was our favorite place to take our dates: the Alcazar theatre, an air-conditioned movie house where, in the early evenings, we could enjoy the latest American flicks in plush seats that, in the darkness, mysteriously sprouted hands that somehow found their way to your girlfriend's chest.

But the main event would take place on Saturday nights, when young people, including yours truly, would don our best *jelga*, or threads, to walk around and to flirt with the opposite sex.

My *jelga* was provided by my mother in New York. She would send me, perhaps out of a sense of guilt in stuffing me into my grandparents' house, the latest in New York fashion—Xavier Cugat shirts—loose-fitting shirts with wide pockets and pleats of a different color running down the front sides, the kind that jazz musicians sported at concerts in those days—*tubitan* pants, heavily pegged at the cuffs and with saddle stitches on the sides, and black-and-white or brown-and-white cordovans.

In fact, my sartorial elegance had, on one occasion, created quite a stir in the Caguas plaza one Saturday evening, when the carousel of boys and girls twirled around each other, the girls rotating clockwise and the boys counterclockwise. We were supposed to throw the girls *una flor*, a verbal flower, such as, "Happy are the eyes that see you, and happy will I be to meet you," or some such sentiment. If the girl whom you passed in the counterclockwise carousel liked your *flor*, she might let you accompany her on her clockwise rotation, to the jeers of your former fellows, now walking in the other direction and cat-calling you as they passed. I was not that adept because, as an *americanito*, I had not yet mastered the intricacies of the *flor*.

Sometimes the khaki contingent from the *titere* (hoodlum) neighborhoods of Caguas, from Savarona or el Verde, came to the plaza to pick fights with the more elegant boys, the *flanes* of the town; I was, perhaps, the ultimate *flan*. The vitriolic jeers from their perches in the trees that lined the outside perimeter of the plaza were a cacophony of crows gone wild.

I finally decided to take my cousin's advice: if you couldn't beat them with your fists because they were bigger or had you outnumbered, well, there were always rocks. So, under the shade of the flowering palm, I stuffed my pockets with stones. When the human crows began their chortling choreography at the next pass, I unleashed a barrage of rocks that had them scrambling and falling from their perches like abandoned pigeons from their nests. They quickly regrouped and started to give chase, their khaki shirts flags flying in the wind. My girlfriends, Tonita la Negra and Gladys, and I flew ahead of that khaki wind through the streets of Caguas and down Vizcarrondo to the safety of our own neighborhood, at whose edge the khaki phalanx came to heel, bare-heeled and many-toed, like the sheriffs in the old cowboy pictures who come to a stop when the fleeing bandit crosses the sacrosanct state line.

Part VI

A TEENAGER IN NYC

36

Parallel Avenues

When mami moved us to the apartment on Third Avenue and Claremont, right across the street from the Claremont Avenue station of the Third Avenue El, to a railroad flat that adjoined the platform of the station—where you could, if you were daredevil enough, lay a plank from our fire escape and walk directly onto the station without having to pay the dime that was the subway fare in those days but which, many times, I and my *gangita* of adventurers and fare evaders didn't pay anyway (as we would sneak in under the turnstile when the train was approaching the station and steal away on the train toward greener parts of the Bronx, to the fields of wild blueberries, which our leader, Tito, had first discovered, and gorge ourselves on them until our hands, faces, and even our clothes were spotted with blue freckles and our feet waved in the breeze from the branches where we would sit to enjoy the blue ambrosia)—Claremont Park was still an oasis of green, where I ran to as soon our *motetes* were safely settled in the apartment, with my little football to throw into the air and the expanse of grass to catch it in its broad green chest, when the park was still green and had shiny metal fences around its green lawns, before they were stolen by the hordes of heroin addicts that eventually invaded the hood like swarms of locusts, stealing everything they could find to finance their fix and making a dust bowl of the park's greenery.

Third Avenue was where we Puerto Ricans lived, or *hispanos* as we styled ourselves then, in a gesture of solidarity with all the other Spanish-speaking immigrants in New York and to the consternation of the gringos who couldn't differentiate at first sight what kind of *hispanos* we were or from what country we originated, and to whose confusion we added on the census forms by describing ourselves as White if our skin was light and our hair straight, or Black if our complexion was dark and our hair knotty, until they caught on to our game and changed the wording on the form to include non-Hispanic White or non-Hispanic Black.

On the other hand, Fulton Avenue, which ran parallel to Third Avenue for a few blocks, was where the Jews lived at that time, or some of them anyway, before Co-Op City was built and its heavy nets hauled them, like rescued fish, from troubled waters to swim in calmer, clearer streams. Third Avenue was under the El, and its street and tenements were under the shade, in the shadow of the antiquated tracks that rumbled angrily whenever the train lumbered through. Fulton faced the park, and it was bright and sunny, embraced by a necklace of emerald.

You could say that they, *los judios*, and we, *los hispanos*, lived parallel lives on parallel avenues that extended on parallel tracks toward an infinite horizon. The only place where these two tracks met was at P.S. 4 (which, coincidentally enough, stretched from Fulton to Third)—but only seemingly, because the school itself had students on different tracks. The Hispanics, coming from schools in Puerto Rico, with minimal English language skills, and some being older and more mature than the rest, were, to use a tongue-twisting word, curricularly challenged and were placed (do I hear the word "segregated"?) into one classroom with a very brave and dedicated teacher, Mr. Cheriot, who struggled just to keep his classroom in order, which was enforced with the help of some of his more muscular students, like Mateo, who with one glance, could bring the rest of the class into perfect order.

Mateo was older than the rest of us, as he had been repeatedly left back in school in PR, where they did not believe in peer advancement. He was certainly mature enough to have, as rumor had it, already fathered children back in the island.

Los judios, mostly, were further ahead scholastically and would go on to more advanced placement in other and better schools, like Stuyvesant or Science, and from there to higher education, while *los hispanos* wound up in vocational schools, like Aviation, which led, generally, to worthless degrees and dead ends.

There was one place, though, where *los hispanos* excelled: in the school's indoor swimming pool, where we gathered twice a week, naked as peeled bananas, for swimming under the watchful eye of the instructor, Mr. Fingers. *Los hispanos*, coming from a tropical island, a gentle Caribbean sea, and many cooling rivers of crystal clarity, were dolphins in the water, fast and graceful, while others hung at the side of the pool, churning the water with feet like human egg beaters.

37

Julio Reverbero

His name was Julio, but, as the new boy in our class at P.S. 4 in the Bronx—fresh from the *campo* in Puerto Rico and bearing yet the *mancha de plátano* from the old country, and being fat and docile, with a smile like a cat and a cat's haunted eyes—he brought out the malice in the not-yet-fully developed moral intelligence of our pre-teen brains; it was almost pre-ordained, then, that we, who had by now lost some of that original stain, would tease him and make fun of him by calling him Julio Reverbero, after a popular comic on a Puerto Rican radio station who always made us crack up when he introduced himself as *Julio Reverbero, para servirle a usted* (Julio Reverbero, how can I serve you?).

But in our malice we chanted: *Julio Reverbero, te meto el deo y te revoleo como un guineo*, which can be loosely translated as Julio Reverbero, I stick my finger in your hole and twirl you around like a banana. After a while, though, we didn't even have to chant our little made-up rhyme; it was enough just to stick our index finger in his face and twirl it. Even the smallest and weakest of us were not afraid to index him, as he would just respond with a benign feline smile and slink away.

Time, like a river into which you can never step twice, flowed through us and with us, and carried us away from the moorings of our enchanted childhood. As we arrived at the port of our uncertain adolescence, Julio, too, floated downstream with us. But it was a different Julio now; he was no longer fat, he was no longer docile, and the feline meekness of his childhood had transmuted itself with the passage of the stream into a panther-like ferocity.

I was made aware of this on one of those hot Bronx summer afternoons that fray the fibers of your brain as I was coming out to the street from the dingy hallway of our building on Third Avenue, carrying with me heavy tomes of psychology and astronomy, books that were my ballasts in that neighborhood where people were drowning in poverty and deprivation. As I stepped out into the klieg light of the afternoon, there was a gang of Scorpions hanging out with their *chica* followers, sitting on the hood of a car by the curb.

As soon as they saw me with my books, they knew they had a pigeon whose wings they could easily clip. I knew I was done for as they began their menacing approach, a scorpion seemingly of one body and many claws. Books, no matter how weighty and deep, could not possibly match fists pregnant with blunt force. I couldn't retreat lest I be branded a coward.

As I prepared myself to receive the first blow I heard a familiar voice that said, in a stentorian tone, "Lay off, guys!" When the face that was buried in the big *tetas* of the *chica* he was nuzzling emerged, it was Julio, Julio Reverbero, who continued to nuzzle his *chica* with his right hand compressing her *nalgas*, as a child would compress two perfectly shaped balloons, while with the left he gave me the index finger, twirling it around as a gesture, perhaps, of our shared past and that saved me from the Scorpions' bite that afternoon in the South Bronx.

38

There's No Business Like Show . . .

Common wisdom has it that talent is inborn, which to me means that those little nuggets of artistry, intelligence, and or good looks travel in these little *capeira* trains of DNA from one generation's station to the next, and we inherit through our genes some traits that we may boast of as being ours but which, frankly, were passed on to us, like heirlooms, from past generations.

Which brings me to say that having experienced, on a recent trip to Las Vegas to visit my niece, the talent in song and dance displayed by her six-year-old son Manuel, both on a video that he showed us of his performance in his kindergarden class and in his live performance for us, I was reminded of the time when my younger brother Cuco, Manuel's granddad, displayed a similar flair for song and dance. I still have a picture of him at about the same age, banging away with a big smile on his face on the little piano my mother had bought him in the hope of furthering his musical abilities. What I do not have now is that old envy and anger born of sibling rivalry at all the attention and praise he won from people because of his showmanship and Polynesian good looks that I hid, like an unwanted outfit you hide in an old closet, that you do not want others to see.

In any case, my mother was so keen on her son's talent that she took him to a promoter who—with his charms and promises that he would work with the kid and develop his talents to the point where he would go on stage for his class's next musical performance—had my mother sign a contract for what must have been an considerable sum of money. I say considerable, considering that the car my stepfather drove was a Model T Ford, one with a crank that he had to work, while I, an embarrassed teenager, who wished we owned a more up-to-date car (like one with fins in the back, say), would sit in the driver's seat, turning on the ignition while he cranked up the motor.

The day of the grand performance came, and we all piled into the Model T Ford and drove to the theatre and sat in the front seats, eagerly awaiting Cuco's stage debut. The opening act was a kid with a heavy Bronx accent who sang, "Never mind the fish in the market, just mind the price of the fish," followed by other singers and dancers and even a budding magician; number after musical number was applauded by pleased and glowing parents and families, until the final curtain came down with the whole class singing in chorus, but with no Cuco in sight.

My mother, whose face was more visibly shaken than the curtain that was dancing with its folds, rushed backstage to confront the manager as to why her son had not appeared on stage. She was told that he had had a bad case of stage fright and had refused to go on, which Cuco denied, crying and saying that the manager had not allowed him to go on, at which point my mother, whose method of operation was to shoot first and ask questions later—and even, after asking questions, continue to shoot anyway—attacked the promoter with all the fury of a she-bear protecting her cub. It soon became bedlam backstage, and security had to be called in to quell the near-riot. After it was over and we were riding back home in the chug-along Model T Ford, my mother, as she was wont to do after some melee between her and whoever she believed to be the offending party, kept yelling at my stepfather, who had tried to reason things out, as to why he always took everybody else's side but hers.

39

Trading Reps

Mrs. Picardos, our assistant principal, more commonly known to us at P.S. 4 in the Bronx as Pickaxe for reasons that will become obvious, was a slight, slightly stooped, middle-aged woman; actually, she listed to the left, her gait resembling that of a female Atlas seemingly carrying the weight of the world on her shoulders. The weight of the world that she seemed to be carrying was, of course, us; not just the elementary classes of P.S. 4, but more specifically, the eighth graders, the seniors of the school, and to focus this social microscope even further, the rowdy group of class 8-8. The class of 8-8 was the wagging, raging tail-end of the eight grade, with the head, 8-1, being the head of the group academically, and the rest, 8-2 to 8-7, the so-so torso. This was the way classes at P.S. 4 were stratified (please do not call to mind that word that begins with s-e-g). The 8-8 consisted exclusively of newly or recently arrived students from Puerto Rico (please do not call them "transfer students").

The 8-8—rather than 8-1, of which I was a part, or the rest of the eighth-grade torso—was the real heavy load that Pickaxe carried on her shoulders, and a heavy load indeed they were. Their zookeeper-dressed-as-teacher, Mr. Cheriot, a soft spoken *moreno* (in English you would say Black or African American) presided over them with a verbal whip of patois Spanish, but even his fulminations and all his brave efforts at control and containment could not keep the lid on class 8-8, whose students were an immigrant kaleidoscope inverted helter-skelter by social forces.

Some of these 8-8ers, though perhaps academically behind us, were far more physically or socially advanced than us, the 8-1ers; take their leader, Mateo, a young man of herculean proportions, the best swimmer in our school and whose word was the underground law that the rest of us dared not trespass. He was, in fact, Mr. Cheriot's enforcer, and he had a scripted sense of right and wrong that never became a subject of debate among us—although the rumor was, which he sometimes seemed to encourage, that he was already the furtive father of several children left behind on the island.

Luckily, Mateo liked me and seemed to adopt me as one would adopt a protégé, admiring me, perhaps, for my better English, or my better grades, or whatever (in French you would say "*je non sais quoi*"). It was a mighty umbrella of protection that I carried with me through the halls and yards of P.S. 4, and a handy one for me, since I, being bilingual, had become the de facto bridge that connected the head and the tail-end of the classes. In fact, many times my home teacher, Mrs. Nims, would send me with written messages, carefully sealed in pretty envelopes, to Mr. Cheriot, and my appearances with the letters always provoked sneers and loud clapping from the class, which Mr. Cheriot's soft verbal whips could not contain until Mateo rose and, with herculean stares, eyeballed the class down.

But the real enforcer of the school rules was, of course, Mrs. Picardo. When we espied her coming down the hall in her listing gait, her gaze beaming ahead like a laser about to burn, we scurried like roaches that had seen the light. She was ever-present in the yard, either outdoors in the summer or indoors when we lined up for the day's classes, and as she went by, each row of students immediately straightened up, as though an invisible iron was straightening out the creases in a wavy garment. If you were late for school (god forbid you were late for school), there she was, in your face, a modern Torquemada of the enhanced interrogation techniques. Our only defense was irony, humor, as when she was followed by two or three boys who she was leading to some disciplinary action or other and they followed behind her in mock listing to the left side, like ducklings imprinting on a lame mother duck.

So it came as a great—no, an astounding and astonishing—surprise to us, all eight classes of the eighth grade of P.S. 4, when, a few weeks before our coming graduation (for some a graduation to academic high schools, others to vocational high schools, still others to the school of the street, to whose corresponding parts of our student body I will let the reader guess), Mrs. Picardo took us in hand, taught us how to dance the foxtrot, the cha-cha-cha, and the waltz, to whose magnificent strains we swooped through the aisles at our graduation exercise in all our dressy finery, with Mrs. Picardo on the piano, her shoulders perfectly straight and her eyes beaming, not with incandescent discipline but with pride and joy at what she and we had accomplished together.

40

Trading Work Ethics

I started my working life (that's a great term, "working life," and like similar terms—the drinking life or the sex life—it usually connotes a momentous shift in one's existence) at around the eighth grade, when my stepfather, Joe, got me a job delivering clothes for Herman Spiegel, known as Hymie, a tailor who owned a tailoring and dry-cleaning shop on 49th Street just east of Third Avenue, across the street from the famous Manny Wolf's, one of the most expensive and exclusive restaurants on the East Side.

To get to Hymie's I took the Third Avenue El at 174th Street, a block down from my school, straight down to 49th Street. It was a juggly, noisy but convenient ride, not only because of its directness but also because it allowed me to hang out by the open door with the gate in the last car of the train and feed my nascent nicotine habit *a lo escondido*, furtively. Sometimes, when waiting on the platform for my train to come, I would catch sight of Maria, a freckled, wide-eyed Italian beauty with flaming red hair, who would open her window and let her lovely face—with lush red lips that could have graced a lipstick commercial and a shower of freckles on her face that only made her more attractive to me, similarly drenched by the same hormonal rain—compete with the bright sun of golden afternoons for my attention. Rarely were any words exchanged between the two of us, either by the station or in the classroom, and the secret crush I carried for her was just that: crushed by my hopeless despair at ever being able to cross the invisible line that separated our ethnic groups from each other.

Working for Hymie, delivering clothes to plush East Side addresses—places like the Waldorf, or the Pierre, or exclusive town-houses whose kitchen spaces were bigger than the entire railroad apartment on Third Avenue and Claremont Parkway where I lived with my parents, with elevators that ascended to dining rooms with mahogany furniture so grand they must have left a gaping hole in the jungles in the Philippines (where, incidentally, my stepfather was from), and living rooms that looked like sets from Hollywood movies of the 1930s—was for me a wide eye-opener, like stepping out of an old closet into the Taj Mahal. However grand these mansion-like dwellings were, though, their occupants typically tipped meagerly, and the most I could get from the service staff who attended me there were dried-out cookies or a piece of stale cake. I generally got bigger tips from the working-class folks who lived in the surrounding neigh-borhood around Third Avenue, where the poor Irish generally lived.

From Hymie, whom I remember fondly, I learned some key les-sons about how the capitalist system works, at least on the level of the working class.

I soon noticed that Hymie charged a lot more on the tailoring and dry-cleaning work that he did for the rich on Park Avenue, the ones with the hot-and-cold-running maids, than he did for the poor Irish in the tenements that reeked of boiled cabbage in the late afternoons when I delivered their clothes; even if I held my nose closed when entering their halls, I always left my pockets open for their tips. When I queried him about this, his reply was that the rich had more money than they knew what to do with, and he was only helping them out by overcharging them.

I learned this lesson so well that when he gave me money for delivery by cab to his uptown affluent clientele, I would take the bus instead and pocket the change. When he queried me upon return why I had taken so long, I would sigh that the traffic on Third was just horrible, horrible. And when his eyes blinked rapidly at this, I would just fluff it off as the effect of the smoke from the cigarette he had wedged between his lips 24/7. After all, he made more money than me, so I was just helping him out.

Another lesson I learned from Hymie was a more personal one. Close to my graduation from P.S. 4, on a special Saturday, Hymie and his wife drove me in their new Rambler, one of the first compact cars that came out on the market, to S. Klein, the store on Herald Square in New York City, where they personally helped me select a brand new blue suit for my coming graduation.

I learned other lessons from Hymie, but the last and saddest lesson I learned was that when the Third Avenue El was coming down, and with it my ride from P.S. 4 to work (the landlord of the building where the tailor shop was located, in anticipation that the neighborhood was in the process of becoming more upscale, increased his rent), Hymie had to close up shop, and I lost my job. Hymie didn't show up the last week I worked there but instead sent his father, also a tailor, who muttered something about his son being sick. I suspected, though, that for a hard-boiled guy like Herman Spiegel, it would have been hard for him to show any cracks in his outside shell, and though I didn't know then the concept of closure, I did feel that I had been cheated out of saying goodbye to Hymie, who I still remember furiously blinking from the smoke of the cigarette he always had wedged between his teeth.

41

Religious Tourists
(to be read in one breath)

Me and my buddy Bolitres—we called him Bolitres as a joke because
he was always coming up with different types of wrestling moves to
show us, which in Spanish are known as *bolitres* and which he learned
from his older and bigger brother when they wrestled in their apart-
ment next to ours, from where we could hear the thuds of their tussles
on the mattresses they laid out on the floor, cleared of all their living
room furniture—the same brother whose wife, Nilda, he stole and
began to live with in concubinage that he justified by saying he was
saving her from the beatings his brother gave her on a regular basis and
that we also heard from our apartment as Nilda was banged around
from pillar to post as he kept calling her a *puta* or whore (which I
secretly knew from my own experience to be true, as one evening she
invited me over to their apartment, supposedly to help her compose a
letter to the IRS but which wound up with my hand down her *pan-
taletas* and into the squishy part between her legs, but then I quickly
fled back into the safety of my own home in a premonition, and before
I closed the door I heard the *swoosh* of the front door downstairs of
the walk-up building, and heard his heavy steps coming up the stairs
[*Ay dios mio, de lo que me he salvado*] because surely the one whom
my parents would have heard being knocked around in the next-door

apartment would have been me, without the safety net of any mattress on the floor), and their mother, Dona Clotilde, was scandalized at the brotherly transfer of the bride, and her tears flooded her face like the tears of the bloodied Jesus on the cross that she worshipped at the masses she attended daily—when he and I were still adolescents and virginal, and he tall and lanky and having not yet attained the heavy weight he would grow into as an adult and the professional wrestler he would eventually become (which probably accounted for his audacious move on Nilda, although he probably coveted her all along, but now that he could out-wrestle and out-fight him, his older brother was forced to leave his own home in ignominy and shame as the tears of Dona Clotilde bathed the feet of Jesus at the daily masses she attended without fail but with more urgency now, seeking God's salve to her own agony), would visit the many storefront churches in our neighborhood—which had proliferated to as many as one or two on each block, casting the shadows of their crosses on the nearby liquor stores, which were just as numerous and as well attended and as full of spirits as their heavenly counterparts—retailers of the Holy Spirit, both the Spanish Pentecostal ones, which featured fat Latina mamas rolling on the aisles and shrieking out in tongues when galvanized by the Holy Ghost (which me and Bolitres imitated later on when a safe distance away, rolling on the sidewalk and spouting as much gibberish as our immature adolescent brains could spin out), and the Black churches, where the mahogany faces of the sweating preachers would anoint us, the religious tourist converts, with aromatic holy oil before we went out and put some distance between them and us and called to each other, "Bro, is you saved?" and danced the jitterbug of salvation, but we enjoyed visiting these retellers of the Word of God, and it was cheaper and more exciting than the movies, and we confessed our sins afterward to Father Xavier and exited from the confessional booth on Saturday evenings with our souls scrubbed clean by the Holy and True Apostolic Roman Catholic Church of Christ.

42

Trading Sexes

What a weird and delightful dream: he was turning into a woman; actually, into a young teenage girl, very pretty, with lovely green eyes and a smooth oval face crowned with short, frizzy hair of the kind that drives boys crazy. And loveliest of all, full, rounded breasts that showed best in the tight little blouse that he proudly donned on the occasion of his coming out. But he wasn't just another pretty girl. His transformative self was actually none other than a beautiful girl who attended the seventh and eighth grades with him at P.S. 4 in the Bronx, and on whom he had a sizable crush, one that was always on hand, to put the matter vulgarly. But if his handy crush was huge, it was definitely dwarfed by the fantasy that his friend Aquino had developed around this girl.

Aquino's fantasy was totally out of control. His every breath and word were exhalations of fantasy love for her; unfortunately, his love was borne in shame and dread, and dared not speak its name to her, although all the rest of us heard nothing else from him. Shame because Aquino was painfully aware of his physical attributes: short, with faint mongoloid features. Dread because he feared rejection if he should confess his true love to her. To make matters worst, this girl was always accompanied by another girl, much less pretty but much more aggressive, who seemed, for most intents and purposes, to be her bodyguard, the guardian of her beauty, the keeper of her solitude, thus keeping us, the fantasizing boys, away.

We were growing into young, young but cautious, adults, as yet not buffeted by the strident winds of the more sexually free Anglo culture that surrounded us, which had not yet the prevailing wind in our little Latino neighborhood; ours, instead, were the gentle tropical breezes of romantic but silent love of which the Trio Los Panchos sang with such plaintive pathos. Though on our jacket sleeves we may have worn gang insignias, our hearts certainly were not displayed there, but languished in dark, hidden places where the guitar weeps.

43

Nilsa

Nilsa's sensuous beauty was such that one look from her would be enough to squeeze the pulp out of our teenage hearts, and her lips, in their ruby ripeness, seemed to say, "Don't worry about the pulp; I'll suck your rind and spit the priapic pits into the cool, blue sheet of the night." In contrast, Rafi, her kept man, had a face that seemed to have run into a cobweb of acne; tall and lanky but nevertheless a fearsome presence, his main pleasure, other than giving us dark looks that warned us not to mess with Nilsa (no free candy, he would say), was to take us on scalabrious rides on the handlebars of his racing bicycle through the narrow gaps between the cars choking the streets of Claremont Parkway until the pumping in our coronary arteries matched the fierce pumping of his legs and the demented laughter that our screams brought out in him.

Mami, on the other hand, neither feared Rafi nor drooled over Nilsa, and when Nilsa moved the site of her operations to the same fifth floor of the walk-up apartment building that we lived in on Third Avenue, and men began congregating like lusting locusts on the stairways and hall that led to her apartment (from where loud salsa music blared into the scarlet hours of the night), mami, fearless moral warrior that she was, complained to the landlord (who lived on the ground floor and whose wife was Nilsa's cousin), and, not getting any results, began to raise a ruckus of her own against the ruckus that was going on on our floor.

When Rafi came out to defend the little tatters of honor that Nilsa might still possess and the honeyed business that lent its sweetness to his livelihood, my mami began to slap him, and he retreated into the red light district of their apartment, shouting that he was not about to hit a woman. As he retreated, the landlord's wife, in defense of her cousin, came up the stairs like a cat ready to fight, with threats and nails bristling, but before she could reach the landing on which mami was waiting for her, mami unleashed a swift karate-like kick that caught her flush on the chest and sent her sprawling against the wall of the staircase. End of bout; TKO in the first round, except that in trying to separate the combatants, the would-be referees, my stepfather included, wound up with their own cobwebs of scratches on their arms and faces.

My girlfriend, Evelyn, who had arrived just in time to witness the fight (she had come with her gay brother, Jerry, and an older couple to pick me up to go to the movies with them) kept repeating afterward amid giggles, "Wow, I didn't know your mother was such a good fighter. Where did she learn to kick like that?" in that sexy and endearing manner that had stolen my heart (which she later crushed, like a cigarette butt crushed underfoot, leaving the scattered pieces to heal in whatever way they could).

44

The Walrus Men

They hung out at the corner of Third Avenue and Claremont Parkway, *hablando mierda* (arguing or bullshitting), waving in the air their beers camouflaged in little brown paper bags, higher in the air when highlighting a point, and then down in a gesture, like coming to a conclusion to their argument, guys a little older than me, who, often coming off the bus that brought me back to the block from William Howard Taft High School, would be forced to make my way through the cluster of big-waisted and semi-wasted men who, like a colony of male walruses on some outcropping of rock by the shore, kept jostling and bumping each other with their ballooned bellies. The belly-bumping was to secure for the guy with the biggest and most aggressive belly—which, if you dared squeeze, would feel like a sponge holding mucho liquid—the center of the circle as the alpha male. But it was constant bumps and push, belly to belly, beer held on high or coming down, and as I made my way through, they would cede me a narrow passage and greet me cordially, and look at the books that I carried under my arm, and smile sympathetically, and hail me with, "Yo, Einstein, cool, man, cool," and then resume their choreography of bumping and pushing and *hablando more mierda*.

They kind of admired me as a serious student in high school, even though they may have short-circuited their own school careers with truancy or delinquency and had dropped out or had been expulsed, so I represented to them, I guess, someone who had made a choice that they had not been able or willing to make, and now they were either sponging from their women on welfare or collecting unemployment benefits from jobs that they held in the winter for just enough weeks to qualify for benefits in the summer and bask in the luxurious sun of the South Bronx, or even from odd jobs here and there, *chiripas* they called it, just enough for beer money.

This one particular time, as I squeezed my way through the colony of these walrus men on the street corner, I was headed for Don Emilio's bodega with a list of groceries that my mother had given me in the morning to pick up at the store on my way back from school and that I was carrying in one of my shirt pockets; in the other pocket lay pieces of scrap paper with the numbers and calculations I had used for a math test that day. Mami had instructed me to tell Don Emilio to put the groceries on her credit bill, which was a running account she had at the store and that which she would pay at the end of the week when my stepfather, Joe, would get his pay check. I could never understand, until that afternoon, why mami couldn't just pay cash for her purchases, but then I extrapolated from one of the test questions I had answered in school that once you start a rolling account of credit, it's tough to get on top of the curve again. I presented the list to Don Emilio, who, like the walrus men barking on the street corner, admired me for my efforts to try to escape from the downward spiral that had already engulfed so many of my contemporaries in the hood.

As he was filling the order, I felt a tightening of the mood among the people in the store as the door was heard opening. Plainclothes police pushed in in pursuit of the *bolitero*, or "numbers man," who used Don Emilio's store as one of his way stations. But the *bolitero* had long since gone, and in their frustration, the police began to harass everyone inside. When he got to me, the lead detective noticed I had a piece of scrap paper with numbers written on it sticking out from my shirt's front pocket, and as he pulled it out and examined it, I suddenly had my own personal experience with the "stop and frisk" policy of the police, which was common practice in the South Bronx long before it had even been given a name as the official policy of the NYPD. I could glimpse the emergence of the "I gotcha look" in his eyes, like I was the *bolitero* he had been searching for. He questioned me as to what I was doing with this list of numbers but shook his head in disbelief as I tried to explain to him that it was scrap paper from a math test I had taken in school earlier.

It was plain to me as the plain clothes he wore that he intended to arrest me, *me*, a budding young scholar on the brink of being mistakenly arrested as a numbers dealer, until Don Emilio, standing by the meat-chopping block and enraged at the injustice taking place, started rattling the heavy butcher knives and cleavers in a loud, threatening manner, muttering angry words denouncing the cops, at which point the detective, sensing that the atmosphere in the bodega had now shifted against him, backed off and exited the store but not without a loud warning that he would be back, indeed, yeah, he'd be back. Whether he came back or not I do not know, but since that day I do all my math calculations in my head.

45

Papo's Odyssey

"Hey, Toño," my little brother, Cuco, said to me, "guess who I saw the other day?"

"Who?" I replied.

"Papo, man. And guess what?"

"What?"

"He's turned, man."

"Turned? How?"

"He's turned gay. A real *pato*, man, *plumas* and everything."

"Papo, man, of all people"

Yeah, Papo, of all people, the toughest, most macho gangbuster of Claremont Parkway, he of Indian-like features, mohawk-style hair, Comanche nose, and hooded eyes that would dart everywhere at once, seeking their visual prey and holding them with a serious, no-nonsense gaze. Papo the dancer, Papo the bongo player, Papo the boxer, Papo the gangsta, who led the Scorpions of Claremont Parkway in turf wars against the Black gangs south of 167th Street, the unofficial boundary separating us, the Latinos, from them, the Boogaloos. Now turned *pato*, with *plumas* no less.

Papo, who would boast of his sexual prowess with the *chicas* that hung around the gangstas like barnacles on rotting seawalls. "Yeah, this *chicha chica*, man, she would beg me, 'go back out and kick the door open, like you did the first time, *que chichamos.*' Man, and I did, I went out, and boom, I kicked the friggin' door open and jumped into her bed, and my *daga* slid into that big *chocha* of hers, like a knife into *flan.*" And we would all laugh, and our own *dagas* would stand in semi-salute to the general of our streets.

Papo, man, whose life I had saved once, when he had been stabbed and was lying bleeding from the ice pick punctures that two of the Boogaloos from below 167th Street had administered to the backs of his knees in treacherous payback, which was the usual MO of gang warfare in the South Bronx. That evening, as I was coming home from a Bible study with Jehovah's Witnesses, I heard a commotion in the entrance of the building where Papo lived. His father and grandmother and wife and children were all screaming, and Papo was lying on the floor of the lobby, bleeding profusely from the wounds in his legs. There was *mucho* wailing, and some of the Scorpions had run down Third Avenue in pursuit of the two Boogaloos that had stabbed Papo with those ice picks, as easy as chipping an ice block but drawing blood instead of water. But no one was helping Papo, whose life blood kept flowing out, crimsoning the raggedy black mat that, ironically, welcomed visitors into the building.

My brain did a swift review of the first-aid class that Mr. O, our Phys. Ed. instructor, had recently given us at Taft High School. "Remember," he had said, his cheeks puffed out and red, whisked perhaps by whiskey and rye, "if the bleeding is in spurts, that means that an artery has been ruptured. In that case, you should apply the tourniquet above the wound, tightening it gently until the bleeding has stopped. However, if the bleeding is a steady trickle, that means a vein has been ruptured, and in that case, you should apply the tourniquet below the wound."

Approaching Papo carefully, sidestepping the congealing puddle of blood surrounding him, I noticed that the blood was coming out in spurts in his left leg, but on the right leg the flow was a steady stream. I asked if anyone had a bandanna or a handkerchief, and, as I seemed like someone who knew what he was doing, half a dozen or so do-rags and kerchiefs were offered to me right away. I quickly applied them as tourniquets, and slowly, miraculously, just like my teacher had said, the blood flow slowly trickled to a stop.

There was still the question of transporting Papo to Morrisania, the nearest hospital. As is often the case in neighborhoods like the South Bronx, the shortest distance from the emergency room and the scene of the emergency is warped by considerations of racism and an indifference to the needs of minority populations; and so we waited, and waited, for the ambulance to arrive. As the waiting lengthened, Papo's father, an intimidating-looking man—who, like Papo, was also into boxing and would often boast in Don Miguel's bodega that, "Yeah, the bigger the man is I am hitting, the more I like it, because I can then punch him *sin pena*"—was becoming more and more agitated, and the two cops on the scene, realizing that this guy was not one to be easily subdued if things got out of hand, folded the bleeding Papo into their car, his father holding tight the tourniquets, and sped away, sirens flashing and lights wailing.

"By the way, he said to say hello to you," my little brother said, and added, with disbelief in his voice, "Isn't that something?"

"Yeah," I admitted. It was something. Papo, once Claremont Parkway's most feared street fighter, now was roaming those same streets sexually homeless, a gender-broken man, easy prey to his former enemies. *Yeah, it was something*, I said to myself, wondering how his sexual compass could have gyrated so violently from its original setting.

From my work as a counselor in a woman's prison, I had become aware of the plasticity of the human sex drive, how its orientation could be altered under stress or duress: incarceration, intimidation, rape. I had seen women, the physically weaker, become the sexual servants of the stronger bull daggers that ruled the prison wards, embracing lesbianism but then casting it away like their green prison uniforms once out of jail, returning to their former straight ways. I had seen others turn under the realization of how men had exploited them and had been, in some cases, the cause of their ruin and incarceration— turn, as it were, to the solace of their same sex.

I had also been made aware, from the rumors that swirled around the corners of Claremont Parkway and Third Avenue like litter in the wind, that Nilda, Papo's wife and the mother of his three little girls, had been having an affair for years with a *medico* at Morrisania Hospital in exchange, the rumor went, for free medical treatment for her children. A mother's bargain, it was said to be, a poor mother's bargain, like the many bargains some of these impoverished women made, their bodies in lieu of back rent, or the tabling of the *bodegue-ro*'s tab, or for another hit of the crack pen. So Nilda, with her soft, cushiony woman's body and breasts of billowing sexual joy, must have made that bargain, and Papo, the street fighter, must have, at some point, discovered that Faustian bargain that loosened his manly wrists. That knowledge must have broken his heart, for he loved Nilda with a crazy but undeniable love.

46

Testing, Testing

"The Iowa State achievement tests are coming, the Iowa State achievement tests are coming," announced Mrs. Bardos, the home room teacher for our eleventh-grade class at William Howard Taft High School in the Bronx, and she wanted us to be mentally and physically prepared for these tests, which were designed to measure the achievement level of high school students throughout the nation and to improve, if necessary, the teaching curricula throughout.

Mentally, we should try to do our best on the tests, she said, and physically, we should get a good night's rest before the test, wear loose clothing, and bring two No. 2 lead pencils for the test. I did get a good night's rest the night before, and brought with me the required lead pencils. As to the loose clothing, I wore my usual signature hip clothing that marked me out as a cool Latino: black denim pants, a cherry pink shirt with the busts of little black horses stamped on it, moccasins, and yes, on my forehead, perched like a proud rooster, a pompadour glistening with shiny pomade in imitation of the style made popular by Tony Curtis, the then-reigning King of Cool.

Not that I was all about being cool or hip, as I also fancied myself as a budding scholar: I subscribed to *The New York Times*, which was duly delivered to my home room desk every morning before the start of class, together with a small container of milk and a chocolate chip cookie, for which I paid ten cents whenever my mother could dig a dime out of her skimpy pocket, and consumed the milk and cookie while consuming the latest world and national news in the paper that featured "all the news that's fit to print." (Because of my high school subscription to the *Times*, the daily delivery of it to my home when I became an adult, and even searching for it whenever I go on vacation, I always tell people that if Plato once said that an unexamined life is not worth living, then I say that a day without *The New York Times* is not worth it, either.)

My favorite feature of the *Times* came on Monday mornings, a two-page magazine entitled "Student News in Review," which, in addition to news that would be of interest to students like me, also featured a section to improve your speed reading by having articles that noted the approximate time it would take you to read a certain section of numbered words, so you could gauge your reading speed and improve it with every week's issue. I got pretty good at it, and estimated that I could read a *Times* article, which were sometimes challenging to read, at the speed of about five hundred to six hundred words per minute. This was before Evelyn Wood, with her speed-reading techniques, was known to the public, and I got to boast later on, when she became popular, that I was the one who taught her how to speed read. (You can tell by this pompous boast of mine that I was not a shy closet intellectual.)

I showed up at the Iowa State achievement test site, which was held in the school's auditorium, as the whole tenth and eleventh grades were being tested, in my hip Latino outfit and my gleaming pencils, and quickly set out to demolish the test. And I mean *demolish* it.

While other students sat in their seats chewing on their pencils and hoping somehow that their chewed pencils would provide the correct and speedy answers, I devoured whole paragraphs like a python devouring a pig, and regurgitated the literary answers with the speed Evelyn would have admired.

When the results came back, Mrs. Bardos, who was a kind and gentle person aging a bit around the edges, called me to the back of the room to go over the results of my test and provide me with a little counseling and guidance. "Well, José," she told me, I had scored mostly in the 95–99 percentile on the test, and, as she showed me from the IBM punch card she held in her hand, there were some sections in which my scores had gone off the chart, meaning that I had out-achieved the parameters of the tests.

My pride swelled with how well I had done and how Mrs. Bardos was encouraging me to continue to go on to higher education; I was "college material," as she phrased it. But if the sail of my pride had been inflated by these words, her next advice to me quickly deflated them. She advised me that I was hanging out with the wrong friends, ne'er-do-wells that had nothing to add to my standing, and that my clothes marked me as perhaps a "hoodie" and that maybe I should change my style, "tone it down a bit," she said.

I didn't really care what she had said about my friends the ne'er-do-wells, since I just hung around them because they were the school toughies and I felt protected inside their friendly cocoon, but her remarks about my clothes and style and her suggestion to tone it down did not sit well with me. Didn't she realize that in the hood where I lived, you had to have swagger and a tone to your style if you were not to be cut by the sharp edges of the people who lived there? Didn't she know that the threads I wore were the outfit that the young dudes in my neighborhood wore as they strutted about in the Latino mating game? Didn't she know that in addition to my school self I also had a self that had to take root and flourish in a neighborhood where style and courage were more important that intellectual achievement? I realized then that in fact she didn't know these things about and around me, and I walked away quietly from my little conference with her with pride mixed with disappointment.

47

My High School Picture

Of the four copies of my high school picture, one in particular presents a very handsome version of me, making me better-looking than I really was, enhancing my good features and de-emphasizing my least desirable ones—not that I have many of those, all modesty aside. It enhanced my appearance by softening some of my features, making my face softer, more serene, slightly more feminine, more like Tony Curtis than Burt Lancaster, while at the same time erasing my freckles, which, in reality, had resisted all efforts on my part to eradicate, including smearing my face all over with lemon juice like I was some kind of margarita drink. Naturally, this was the photograph that was included in the William Howard Taft High School yearbook in 1959, which, like all things perishable—including my photo—have by now been broken down into atomized particles of cosmic-matter dust, scattered throughout the universe by the winds of time. Nevertheless, this was also the photo I sent to my relatives in Puerto Rico, hoping to thereby impress them with my photogenically glamorized self.

That summer following graduation, my mother, like she did practically every summer, took me and my younger brother with her to Puerto Rico, to visit and stay with my grandparents in Caguas and become reacquainted with the language and the culture that had formed her completely and was forming us only partially as *newyorricans*. Two of those relatives were my uncle Manuel and his wife Carmen.

When I first visited them, Carmen was alone in the house, and when I asked for tio Manuel, she replied cynically that he was on and about the town, displaying the photograph that I had sent them and playing his usual role of Lothario, trying to impress some girls with it, which he hoped would provide a bridge that would lead to their interest in him. It seemed to me that over the years, as Carmen had grown more layers of fat on her body, she had also added layers of cynicism to her outlook, but knowing how my tio Manuel operated, I was not about to argue with Carmen about his displaying my photo all over town hoping that he would indeed interest some good-looking Caguena with it and thereby make my sliding back into the Rican dating scene easier, even though I might be swimming in his swelling wake.

I was watering with anticipation at this newly sprouted thought when, as if conjured by my thoughts, tio Manuel appeared on the scene with my picture in one hand and gesturing with the other—in that peculiar gesture that Ricans use to indicate in a polite way that someone should to come closer: the palm turned downward and the four neighboring fingers of the thumb flexing—to two gorgeous Caguenas who were following him to come into the house.

This was to be the first test of the power of photography when it bumps up against the hard shoulder of reality, and I could instantly sense that for the better-looking of the two Caguenas, there was a déjà vu of mismatch: the *mi cuerpo presente* (reality) could not match the *cuerpo* presented in the photo. But this by no means prevented tio from continuing to sing my virtues—what a fine student I was, what a bright future I had in front of me, and so on—until finally, from sheer embarrassment, I started to leave the house. On my way out I heard tio begin to strum his guitar, and I realized that his sales pitch had now taken a musical turn; Lothario was morphing into Orpheus.

Part VII

MAMI

48

The Medium

Mami was *una espiritista*, a spiritualist or medium, who could summon the spirits of the underworld to appear and speak with the help of human voices and to communicate with us mortals about their spiritual existence and to provide help or succor as needed. She did this at an altar she had built in the last room of our apartment on Washington Avenue in the Bronx with a table that contained a large bowl filled with water through which *los espiritus* had to pass to cleanse themselves of any contaminants from the netherworld and that made the water in the bowl swirl and take on an a cloudy appearance.

On the table were also small idols of *las siete potencias africanas*, or the seven potentates of the Yoruba religion, including, in one corner, an oversize icon of Chango, the mischievous god of the Yorubas, dangling a cigar in his mouth, which mami would light so Chango could smoke and clear the air of impurities; on an opposite corner and facing Chango was an oversize icon of the dusky Santa Barbara. These were the two spiritual and physical guideposts that signified the spiritual union of the Catholic and Yoruba religions. A large cross with the body of the crucified Jesus hanging on the wall in front of the table dominated the scene, in further testament to the hybridization that was the foundation of *el espiritismo* as practiced throughout the Caribbean, the South Bronx, and everywhere else Chango met Jesus Christ.

On the table lay a book entitled *El Evangelio Segun el Espiritismo*, or the Gospel According to Spiritism, which, one day, when out of curiosity and out of mami's sight, I happened to pick up and start to read. I began to have intellectual shivers and chills as the author, whose name I have since forgotten, converted every saying made by Jesus and every scene in the Gospels as enacting a spiritualist session or lesson.

Jesus is said to have cast out legions of spirits and demons that had possessed men and women, and had made them either spiritually or physically sick; mami, in her séances, summoned the equally malevolent spirits that were causing pain or illness. After forcing them to identify themselves and 'fess up their role in that or this person's illness, she would convince them to cease from making this or that person ill. It was not an easy job, as some of these spirits were resistant to be exorcised from the human body that they had possessed, and some of them would take revenge by trying to gain possession of mami's body, which went into convulsions as the spirits entered her. But mami, with the help of Chango and Santa Barbara, was always able to overpower them and send them back to the dark abyss with much fanfare and words of constriction, which they expressed through the mouths of their human hosts. These herculean efforts would exhaust her, and she would faint or fall into a trance, and then we would minister to her with cold compresses and rubbing *alcolado*.

At times, mami would say that I had the gift to become an *espiritista* myself and would encourage me to take up the art of what she called *la magia blanca*, or white magic, which she said was what she practiced to help others in trouble or pain—but I would not have any of it. I didn't want any *espiritus* looming over my bed, and I slept with my feet tightly coddled under my bedsheets so that no *espiritu* could grab me by my toes.

There came a time, though, in which I asked her for her help. I was in college, and when I came home, our living room was often packed with young, nubile Latinas who had come to mami with lovesick problems or seeking potions she prepared that would cast a romantic spell on their recalcitrant boyfriends. In addition to these potions, she would—as she had an acute psychological sense of people's characters—dispense advice on their affairs, and they would leave, a lot happier, with the potions and the verbal therapy mami administered.

"Mami," I said to her one day, "can't you prepare one of these potions for me to *get* close to some of these beautiful women?"

Looking at me with the wise eyes of an ancient wizard and a smile at my boldness in asking her to exercise her magic on my behalf, she replied, "Don't worry, I see a bright romantic future ahead of you."

Oh, well, I can't say I didn't try.

49

Behind the Green Door

Batavia was one of those small towns in Upstate New York with boring, narrow stores and a single dilapidated movie house. In the sixties, it looked so like the back set of a Hollywood Western that you sometimes expected clumps of tumbleweeds to come sweeping by, and its young people were so bored that even those would have constituted something worth rapping about.

It was no surprise, then, when my cousin Raquel disappeared, according to some witnesses, on the back of a motorcycle headed for the Big Apple. Of course, New York City had not been repackaged as the Big Apple yet; that would come later, under the management of more tourist-minded city elders like Mayor Bloomberg, whose very name serves as an onomatopoeia of the eventual reblooming of the city. This was the only clue that my family in Batavia had about the disappearance—or perhaps kidnapping—of my cousin.

She had been missing for several months, and her parents were frantically at their wits' end. The police had treated this case not as a missing person case but as a runaway, and were therefore not giving it a high degree of priority. They had better things to do than spend too much time on these cases.

Confronted with the inertia and lack of action by the police in Batavia, Raquel's parents came to the Big *Manzana* to plead with my mother to employ her powerful psychic powers and help them find their sixteen-year-old daughter. Mami possessed, and sometimes was herself possessed by, a wide embrace of spiritual tools at her disposal: *las siete potencias africanas*, which included all the African deities of the Yoruba religion—such as Chango, the most revered of these *siete potencias*—who had transmigrated intact from the "dark continent" by means of mediums like mami; her spiritualist handbooks and bibles; her séances with the dead and spirits of the underworld; her white magic and her innate ESP powers. She was, in short, a psychic powerhouse, loaded with these invisible tools like a Con-Edison guy with all his paraphernalia strapped on.

The psychic arrows pointed their valences toward Brooklyn, a borough more or less contained within the boundaries of the Brooklyn-Queens Expressway. So, in my uncle's Cadillac, heading in the direction the *espiritus* pointed mami, the family circled Brooklyn. With the spiritual lodestone of the girl's vibes they left the expressway, circling ever closer to where Raquel would be, her image in mami's mind beaming in like a psychic lo-jack.

Finally, they came to a street, and in that street to an alley, and in that alley to a closed green door. Mami, pointing Rosin to the door of the alleyway, said to her, "Behind this green door is you daughter." When Rosin pushed open the door, there indeed appeared Raquel, a bit emaciated, a bit dehydrated, but eager to return to Batavia and her mother after her enforced captivity.

Great is the joy in heaven when the prodigal daughter is returned! All the angels in heaven and Brooklyn sang paeans of joy at her return, and the drums of the Yoruba deities began their joyful beat in the Afro-Boricua skies.

Que viva Chango, que viva Chango . . .

50

The Séance

"*En el nombre del padre, del hijo, y del espiritu santo.*" With the intonation of these words and the tapping of a pencil on the side of the bowl filled with water and sitting in the middle of the table (the water being the medium through which the *espiritus* from the other world would have to traverse in order to cleanse their souls and wash away their wrongdoings, and the tapping of the pencil on the side of the bowl being the knock on the spiritual door that would summon them to the table), the medium, *la espiritista* (who happened, in this world, to be my mother), began the session. Outside, the summer night sweltered with people, their voices drifting up to my uncle's second-story apartment, indistinct, a bubble-blabber from broken rivers.

As the first spirit passed, the water in the bowl began to fog and form a gyring whirlpool, slowly at first and then more violently, whirling and splashing, and the whole table became convulsed. Its electric energy quickly transferred to Carmen, my aunt-in-law, who became galvanized with the surge that was passing through her.

The spirit, with a huge man's voice, angrily demanded to know who had dared summon it from its peaceful rest, all the while shaking Carmen like a rag doll in the hands of a mischievous child. Mami, in turn, demanded that it identify itself, using the name of Jesus as her verbal badge and authority to make the spirit comply with her demand. The spirit answered by shaking Carmen more viciously, but slowly, as the medium continued to demand an answer and began to recite the Lord's Prayer, Carmen's shaking subsided, the spirit's voice softened, and it began its tale in a pidgin Chinese voice.

It described its noble Chinese pedigree from some undecipherable dynasty and how, in its earthly life, it had met an untimely death at the hands of its enemies. But the medium was not satisfied, and her interrogation began to wear the spirit down. It confessed that its Chinese pedigree story was a lie, and when it confessed its more lowly antecedence, the medium, satisfied now as to its true nature, gave it permission to return to its netherworld abode. (Mami would later explained to me, as though I were her sorcerer's apprentice, although I had not the slightest inclination to summon people from the dead—when, in fact, I had trouble enough summoning up a girlfriend from the living—that spirits are liars, big-time fabricators that would make up grandiose stories about the earthly past and had to be tamed and made to confess their real natures and deeds—a kind of spiritual parole clemency board.)

On this night we were in the full throes of a spiritual agenda. One of the recalcitrant spirits that had been summoned in a fit of rage from the bowels of the netherworld seized one of the other participants in the session. Rodrigo, who was seized by the spirit fury, ran to the window and was about to leap therefrom—to land, probably, on the young crowd below and on their jingle-jangle portable radios—if we had not seized him quickly and, with all our collective strength since he was young and very strong, brought him back inside the apartment while mami administered the spiritual chants and prayers that induced this furious *espiritu* to return to the dark stockades of the underworld.

Mami had argued, in trying to convince me to take up the *espiritista* role, that I had the "gift," by which she meant some of her considerable ESP powers, which I had myself witnessed many times, like when she found my cousin Raquel, who had gone missing from her parents' home in Batavia.

Regardless of whether I had the gift or not or whether mami was just saying that in order to start a mother-and-son spiritualist business, I was frankly terrified of being visited in the middle of the night by creepy ghouls or to have visions of a dreadful future, like the time when the spirits announced to her, before the cops knocked on our door, that her brother had suffered a serious car accident, which sent her into a spiritual malaise marked first by dreadful screams and then by a fainting swoon from which she had to be physically revived by smelling salts.

I was in college when mami made her offer, which I declined, naturally; I was satisfied with coming home from classes at the City College of New York (CCNY) and socializing with some of the more luscious Spanish girls that came to mami's apartment seeking spells and love potions to advance their romantic agendas.

51

Trading Names

He was, by all accounts, a good union steward at the Bronx hospital where my mother worked: hardworking, honest, dedicated. But he was also a bit of a *relajon*, meaning that he was always joking around; his specialty was in giving people nicknames, nicknames that were so apt that they stuck like verbal tattoos. Like, for example, when he nicknamed Pancho, the porter in the clinic, Bolitres because he was into wrestling and wrestling holds, called in Spanish *bolitres*, or baptized Chago with the name Pinche because he was always pinching (lifting) stuff from others. So why was he so upset with Dona Rosa, my mother, the one person who, out of respect and maybe a little fear, he did not attempt to nickname?

"Dona Rosa," he came to complain to her at the housekeeping department where she worked, "all the guys are calling me Obispo; Obispo this and Obispo that, and I found out that it was you who gave me that nickname. Now I'm known as Obispo, and I'd like to know why you did that."

"Well, now," my mother said, hiding a sly smile under the dust broom she used for dusting the office furniture. "What does an *obispo* do? Isn't the bishop the one who doles out Christian names to the faithful at confirmation? And aren't you the one who has been doling out nicknames to everyone around here, Señor Obispo?"

Actually, his new label of Obispo did not turn out badly for the union leader; it added a patina of respect to his already excellent reputation with his union members and humanized him to them in a small measure. The new nickname was his card of entry into the brotherly club of those whose personas had been rebaptized according to their earthly desserts.

52

Trading Faces

When you live in a Puerto Rican household, the *botanicas* are not very far away, nor are the spirits, either, for they linger, at night, in the air, sometimes brushing against your feet if you are foolish enough to sleep with your bare feet protruding out from your blanket.

"The way to tell the difference between real and spirit beings," mami said, "is to look at their feet, for *los espiritus* have no feet but float on air without the need of feet."

La fiesta that night was lively and gay, and celebratory: celebratory of the fact that our community had recently escaped the clutches of the poverty that gripped Puerto Rico like a vice shortly after the end of the war. And, although soon we learned not to expect money to fall like manna from the sky onto streets paved with gold, money for fiestas and good clothes and rum flowed from the labor of the family, who all worked, coincidentally, in Mr. White's restaurant. Mami worked the cash register, and my uncles were busboys, dish washers, and cooks.

But mami said that you shouldn't laugh too loud or have too much fun, for in the yin and yang of the universe, life seesaws between joy and pain, and your descent into the bottom of the abyss will be commensurate with the height achieved in the moment of your greatest happiness. Therefore, that night of the party, sometime into the night after the party had ended but before the police had arrived, we were all awakened by mami's soul-searing screams, her premonition, which *los espiritus*, who float about without the need for feet, had brought to her the news of the terrible car accident that her brother Manuel and his small group of revelers were to suffer on a wet road glistening with the dew of alcohol.

Before that horrible car accident on that rain-slicked bridge that destroyed his face, tio Manuel was quite a gallant, a "gay blade" in the parlance of those days, *un macho Latino muy macho.*

He had a very handsome face and a beautiful singing voice, was *romantico* and woman-prone; often, tio was cajoled by one of his enamored friends to provide *una serenata* to their obscure object of desire. After the serenade, when the obscure object of desire's heart had been melted by the sound of his voice and the canto of the guitar, and reshaped so that its form tilted toward tio and away from the original suitor—who would stalk away angrily, hopefully not in search of a blade—and after the obscure object of desire's father had come out with his cannon to threaten tio with, and after tio had looked down the barrel of that gun, giving it his best pose as to the eye of a camera, and after that guardian's guard had been let down and he brought out a bottle of Ron Cañita to toast what he forecasted as the *honrada* thing to do (a formal courting, an engagement), tio was nowhere to be found after he had done the *deshonrada* thing to do and fled away with the *honra* of the obscure object of desire, fled away to sing another day.

But that glistening abutment of that Madison Avenue bridge, whose reverberations traveled on psychic waves to beat paeans of pain in my mother's heart, changed all of that forever. He was in the *matadero* for a long time, what seemed like an eternity to my child's mind, so long that his face and his voice began receding from my mind, until one day he reappeared again, his face wrapped in gauze like the face of the Invisible Man in the movie. And then one day the gauze came off, and I could not look, afraid that his face had vanished. But it had not vanished. Scars had formed, now filled with tiny rivulets of tears that streamed down his face and fell with the sound of silence on the chords of an invisible guitar.

Part VIII

A YOUNG MAN IN NYC

53

A Clash Inside and Outside the Ring

My stepfather, who was Filipino, decided to take me to the fight one night in the old Madison Square Garden in New York City, between the reigning WBC featherweight champ, Flash Elorde, from the Philippines and the number one contender, Frankie Narvaez, who, like me, hailed from Caguas, Puerto Rico. Caguas has produced a lot of good fighters, like Narvaez, a fact attributable to Caguas having one of the best boxing programs on that side of the island.

(But it is also true that many of the kids from Caguas, coming from rough neighborhoods like Savarona and El Millon, like to fight. This fact was driven home to me forcefully when I came back to Caguas to do the seventh grade in junior high school; coming from an easier life in New York City, I was not mentally or physically prepared for the strutting, the challenging, the readiness of my fellow students to engage in the schoolyard version of the manly art of self-defense. And, even though I had read in Hamlet that "rightly to be great is not greatly to be right, but rather, to find quarrel in a straw," my physical condition, which included a serious ear infection from which I suffered since early childhood, did not make me a prime candidate for any type of fisticuffs. Frankly, I was always afraid that any blow to the left side of my head would knock me out of the ring of this world. Luckily, my cousin and hanging-out partner, Chuchin, himself a member of the Caguas boxing club, had my back, often taking the challenge that was meant for me, and as a result of his reputation, these challenges were usually soon withdrawn.)

At the Garden, we had ringside seats of folding wooden chairs that had been hurriedly added that night for the fight as a result of the intense interest it had generated, especially from the large Puerto Rican population in the city. The reader might think at this point, and from the title of this story, that a setup is coming his way, deduce that this is all gearing to be an easy metaphor for the relationship between my stepfather and me. Well, I can assure him that nothing could be closer to the truth because, as a matter of fact, Joe (I called my stepfather Joe, never father, and he called me Toño, never son) was indeed rooting proudly for the Philippine champion, and I, in turn, had an equally passionate stake in hoping that Narvaez would win. It was indeed, as the title suggests, a clash inside and outside the ring. And it did not disappoint.

Flash, true to his name, came flashing out from his corner in the early rounds with swift jabs and a shifty defense, scoring point after point against Narvaez, who kept stalking him, moving forward without apparent concern for the power in Flash's punches, hoping to get underneath the welter of punches to deliver a telling blow, as he was the heavier puncher of the two. In the next-to-last round he delivered a devastating right cross to Flash's left eye, and a geyser of blood gushed up in a perfect ruby-red arc toward the smoky ceiling, like water from an illegally opened fire hydrant in a hot South Bronx street.

Flash's legs quickly became wobbly spaghetti, and the Ricans in the cheaper seats in the upper balconies went into a convention-like frenzy, whooping it up for their candidate, raising crudely lettered signs with Narvaez's name and making the Garden's rafters shake with their demonstrations and stamping of feet. The smell of the crowd and the roar of the blood mingled in a deafening rumble of hopes unloosened, hopes that a Puerto Rican champion was being born. But Flash hung on for dear life and tied up Narvaez in bodily knots in the last round, preventing him from delivering the final coup de grâce.

The decision, ladies and gentlemen, went unanimously to Flash, and just as unanimously and anonymously, beer bottles, empty glass pints of rum, unconsumed food, and other trash came raining down on the ring and those of us around it. From the debris on the floor, a smart marketing executive could easily have constructed a successful sales campaign for the Rican clients in the city: bottles of Schaffer beer, half-pints of Rum Don Q, and Pedro Domecq brandy, all consumed and shattering on the floor. Joe and I, fearful of the crystal rain that was falling down upon us, shielded ourselves with the folding chairs as umbrellas against the crashing debris. Soon the sirens were wailing, and soon the boys in blue were staging their own championship bouts with the unruly Rican crowd until order was restored, one baton blow at a time.

I read in *The New York Times* next morning that as a result of the riot, Madison Square Garden would suspend staging fights in its arena, a ban that lasted for several decades. Joe, amused by the antics of the crowd, agreed with the judges' decision, and I disagreed, because as I had learned in the schoolyards of Caguas, what counts is not the number of punches thrown in a fight but who stands tall and unbeaten at the end, and that, to me, ladies and gentlemen, was, on that night, Frankie Narvaez from Caguas, Puerto Rico, my home pueblo.

54

The Devil's Ontological

He was fertile ground for the preaching of Jan the Witness. A summer or two ago, in Caguas, another Witness had left him a Spanish copy of their little green book *The Truth Shall Make You Free*, which he had leisurely perused while lying on the *hamaca* in his grandmother's hen garden and which had remained on the surface of his subconsciousness like an open book floating on the surface of the water. Jan, a recent convert himself to the Jehovahs, as they were derisively *apelled* by nonbelieving philistines, became very excited at the receptiveness of the young man and the prospect of helping to bring a new, redeemed sheep into the fold of "The Truth."

He left with Antonio an English copy of the book—this one brown—some recent copies of the "Watchtower" and "Awake" magazines, and an appointment to start a Bible study with him next Wednesday at seven in the evening. Jan, a locksmith during the day and a door-to-door Jehovah on weekends and evenings, felt as exhilarated as if he had picked a lock open and was now ready to enter through a door of faith, to the saving of a soul. Glory, Hallelujah!

Many Bible studies later, and after attending Jehovahs meetings— the congregational meetings, the Watchtower study groups, the school meetings—where they were taught the art of public speaking, and after a score of confrontations with his frowning parents, both philistines, a.k.a. Catholics, which only served to reassure him in his faith in The Truth, (as these were only domestic lions that a toothless Satan had halfheartedly sent down to persecute him and test his faith), he, in a lukewarm pool in a Y somewhere in Connecticut, went under the water, a sin-besotted soul going under but a saved, stainless soul rising up, and his sins were washed away by the blood of the Lamb of God, Glory, Glory, Glory be to Him!

Antonio and Jan together began to unlock other people's minds by preaching and preaching and preaching, door to door and door to door, in Gentile, Jewish, Muslim, Black, Latino, ladino, in what-have-you neighborhoods and to what-have-you people, the message of repentance, that Armageddon, the mother of all wars, was about to be unleashed by Jehovah, that the angels and the archangels were already in full metal gear, and that at our back you could truly hear the Eternal Chariot drawing near.

But Satan, that clever dentist, began to sharpen the teeth of the lions back home, and his parents' opposition became stiffer, to the point where an ultimatum was given: either college or the Jehovahs; either leave the religion or leave the home. The ultimatum may have been a ruse, a trick to squeeze him out of the Truth fold, but to Antonio, it signified another thorn on the crown that Jesus was passing on to him, and he took it, and he wore it, and the next day he moved out. First, to Brother Lee's house, who, together with Jan, were his mentors; Lee, whose lore of his Baltimore outlaw days of yore, when he fought duels mano-a-mano with the racist pigs, provided vivid vignettes as sidebars to his biblical instruction, and then to Sister Conchita's house. Lee's place had become overcrowded, seeing that Jan, too, had moved in after being locked out by his Magyar father; altogether another thorn in our collective crown, Glory be to Jesus!

The next day, Antonio moved into his own room in Sister Conchita's house in the Bronx, where she lived with her daughter, Fonseca, or Fonsi for short, who was in her twenties and thus close to his age, and three other rambunctious younger children, who quickly became a threesome following him around. Sister Conchita, or Conchi, had an easy smile and a friendly manner and made him feel very welcome in her home.

It might have been Descartes who first posited the ontological proof for the existence of God: that is, one of the attributes of God is perfection, and one of the attributes of perfection is existence; ergo, God exists or he couldn't be perfect. The devil's own ontological, on the other hand . . .

The bedrooms in Conchi's were upstairs on the second story; Antonio's room was located at one end of the hall and the bathroom at the other, with Conchi's, Fonsi's, and the litters' rooms located in between. On the way to the bathroom that first night, as he was passing by her room, lo and behold, he espied Conchi lying naked on the bed, a vision of breasts refulgent as twin rounded moons on a sparkling sea of flesh, an ancient vibe from Bathsheba's garden resonating in his chest. He stepped into the room, seared by the light, and into the sea, where he drowned.

55

Dancing Dog

It was a ritual of Sunday afternoons in the summers of Crotona Park: Indio, wearing his trademark red bandanna (red for the Scorpions, the Latino gang that reigned over the streets of Claremont and Third Avenue in the South Bronx, of which he was the Defense Minister, meaning that he was the one who arranged the gang fights, usually in this same park, against the White ethnic gangs to our north, the Fordham Baldies, or the Black gangs, to our south, who, for lack of a designated name, we called the Boogaloos because they were always jiving and dancing the boogaloo), he would lug his conga drums to the park to jam with the other *bongoceros* of the hood. The rhythmic beats of the congas, together with the sweet aroma of *hierba*, would waft aloft toward the neighboring fields and buildings surrounding the park, waves of sound that in the beginning drifted across unruly ocean waves from Mother Africa to the Caribbean Isles, rhythms that signaled war, or crop festivals, or just the melancholic moods of one Black man's sorrow, but to us meant joy, movement, spirit, salsa.

I had absented myself from the gang for a while, but not the usual way in which some of our other *gangistas* absented themselves from the *ganga* by doing time or recovering from the blunt wounds of homemade zip guns or going on junkets to the home country but because I had sojourned a while with the Jehovah's Witnesses. For the most part, it had been a good sojourn. I had been embraced warmly to the collective breast of the Witnesses and had achieved—as the Apostle Paul said that he had achieved certain fame among the Jews for his persecution of the early Christians—some recognition in Bible study and public speaking and all the other things that typified the Witnesses. I had even managed to bring into the flock a few converts, who followed me around like I was the Oracle of Solomon: James, the ex-boxer, ex-alkie; Wysbiskie, the Pole and ex-anti-Semite; and some Black and Latino women, some of whom were probably lonelier than they were thirsting for the Word.

At my back I would always hear the rumblings of Jehovah's War of Armageddon drawing near, and frankly, I had been afraid. Afraid not for myself—except for a few strays from the True Path like passionate kissing and amorous stroking of the tender parts of my girlfriend Evelyn's anatomy, or when my eyes creamed at the sight of the folded legs of some of my nubile Bible students, I had stayed mostly on the beam that would someday transport me straight to heaven—but for my family: my mother, my brother, and even my sometimes-mean stepfather, all of whom, having rejected the call to join The Truth, would someday be cut down by the sword of the Archangel Michael and would drift away in a river of blood, to hell or to oblivion. This Witness doctrine would inspire such terror in me that sometimes, while I waited at some subway station and heard the rumble of an unseen oncoming train thinking it was the advance sound of Armageddon, I would tremble at the fact that these loved ones of mine had rejected the life-saving rope that would pull them out of the morass of this soon-to-die world and into the new world of God's creation. Why should they be slaughtered by a merciful God because they saw a different profile of Jesus's face than that which the Jehovahs preached?

In the end, I could not hold this strained position any longer and stumbled backward, to be back again with the Scorpions on Sunday afternoons at Crotona Park, smoking Panama Red and dancing to

Indio's Afro-Cuban beat, and laughing as Indio's dog, Taino, high by contact and wagging his tail, cha-cha-cha'd to the beat of the *clave*.

Los Marcianos llegaron ya
Y llegaron bailando cha-cha-cha-cha
Ricacha, ricacha, ricacha
Asi llaman en Martes al cha-cha-cha.

56

A Reverse Baptism

After my brief, guilt-freckled affair with Sister X, who shall remain anonymous so that the devil, if he be up and about, will have a harder time finding her, I dropped out of the Witnesses and underwent what you might call a "reverse baptism." Whereas in order to officially become part of that congregation of deluded millenialists of Jehovah worshippers I had being dipped in and out of the polluted waters of a river somewhere in Connecticut in my first baptism, my second one was more like an immersion in the turbulent waters of New York's intellectual life. More precisely, of the New York Life Insurance Company, over at Park Avenue in the thirties, where I began to work as a file clerk and to rub intellectual shoulders with college students from sundry New York City schools—NYU, Columbia, St. John's, et. al—both graduate and undergraduate, who also worked there, and whose work consisted mainly of a stream-of-consciousness Socratic dialogue throughout the day, with the filing taking a secondary role and sometimes, if it began to pile up, that went down the porcelain cabinet of the toilet bowl.

For me, a child of the South Bronx, newly emancipated from the yoke of a self-imposed religious obsession, those heady discussions had an intoxicating effect, fine verbal wine consumed by an intellect parched for years, toiling in the desiccated vineyards of an implacable god that had miraged in the deserts of the Sinai. Thirsting for more, I quit New York Life and enrolled in City College as an English major, in which department wordsmiths worked their golden filigrees of iambic pentameters and chains of silvery sonnets, and I quickly fell in with this crowd.

There, in the cafeteria, where we huddled to read our golden poesy, I met Pablo and Rios, two budding poets who would have a life-long influence on my verse, as little and anemic as it has been. Pablo, already a published poet took a Virgilian-like interest in me, trying to inculcate the classical order of rhythm and rhyme into the raw, undisciplined style that marked my writings and which I hope never to lose; Ishmael, on the other hand, grabbed the collar of my prose and dragged it into the wild Harlem of delusional night. Standing between these two opposite poles, I despaired whether the little seeds of poetry that I carried in my clenched fist would ever open and bloom into fertile flowers of creativity.

57

The Bathtub in the Front Room

It was my last year at CCNY, where I was an English major (not a colonel, as the joke went), and I had decided to jump out of the home nest roost on my own, as many of my friends were doing at the time. My apartment was an old, one-bedroom fifth-floor walk-up on Amsterdam Avenue between 88th and 89th Streets with low rent, low enough to be affordable to a CCNY student in the midsixties like me, working part-time at the Engineering Society Library on East 42nd Street, near the United Nations.

It was furnished in the latest style; that is, with the latest furniture that the Hungarian super who lived on the first floor said I could scrounge from whatever serviceable stuff had been left on the sidewalks of the neighborhood on Tuesday night for pickup by Sanitation on Wednesday morning, or whatever had been left behind in their apartments by tenants anxious to beat the marshall on the way in to evict them. The apartment had a wonderful view of the elegant building's blank brick wall in front of my back window, and through a slit between it and another, smaller building, you could see a part of the marquee of the old New Yorker Movie House so that, if you were good at, say, playing the "Movies" category on Jeopardy, you could fill out the rest of the obstructed letters to see what was their current offering.

But the unique feature of the place, its most outstanding selling point from my point of view, was the old-fashioned bathtub in the middle of the front room, standing on short, clawed legs, with a porcelain-like cover over it. It was a great and unique feature, for on Saturday nights I would fill it up with ice and ice all the beer I could buy or my guests would bring to our Falstaff-like revelries. These revelries were heightened to the power of two, as my next-door neighbor, Erica, or Ricky, as she was appelled, would join me in throwing mutual parties. She hosted her friends at her place and I in mine, and the doors of the apartments were left open for the easy mingling of the invited guests.

Unfortunately, the ice in the bathtub could not cool the heated friction that would develop between her crowd and mine. Ricky's friends were of the leftist bent, professed Marxist-Leninists, Maoists, Castro supporters, and other hangers-on. On my side of the mini-Iron Curtain were free-thinkers, poets, artistic types, and a few Korean Veterans (there were always a few Korean Veterans in any sizable gathering of Puerto Ricans in those days).

On her side was a particularly petulant Communist, a very muscular weightlifter known to everybody as the "Marxist strong man," whose muscularity included frequent exercise of the tongue to espouse his leftist ideology; on my side was a Korean Veteran who had been traumatized so much by the war that he saw a Communist hiding behind the label of every bottle of beer.

It didn't take long, unfortunately, for petulance and trauma to rub against each other, and, as the song goes, "You can't light a fire without a flame," soon the flame of verbal controversy began between left and right, and then lefts and rights were thrown, and soon the scene resembled that of a bar fight in a John Wayne cowboy movie. As Ricans say, "*Asi se formo las tangana,*" that's the way the shit went down, with both apartments in an uproar, and the neighbor calling the police, and the police rushing up to break up the fight, and the party dissolving, and afterward, Ricky laughing and saying, "Every great party ends with the police singing the last song."

58

Ricky and the Mad Poet

I had waited way too long to make a move on Ricky, and instead, like the *alcaguete* that I sometimes am, I had delivered her to my drinking buddy, Ishmael, *el poeta loco*. The *alcaguete* role has a long and noble history in Spanish literature and dates back to the time of Lope de Vega, to the Spanish Golden Age, when the *alcaguete* was the formal role of someone, in the archaic role of an internet date service, who arranged for couples to meet and facilitated marriages.

That was what I stupidly did with Ricky and Ishmael. It happened in the cafeteria in City College (I remember it well) when, eager to introduce one to the other—Ricky, a Jewish girl from Englewood Cliffs in New Jersey, who, I am sure, had sneaked her way into CCNY without paying the tuition charged to non-city residents by having her parents set her up in an apartment in the city, though they, from her description of them, had enough money to send her to Princeton or any other Ivy League school, and Ishmael, *el poeta loco* from the Bronx, who intrigued me because of his claim, unlike Joyce's Molly Bloom, who had opted for life, that he had opted for death, although the only death that I could foresee for him was from alcoholic poisoning a la Dylan Thomas—I fell into the role of the alcaguete. (I will no longer italize that word, as a sign of the anger that I feel over missed opportunities.)

Anyway, at that introductory meeting (later on, Ishmael would tell me that the flash of Ricky's mammalian accoutrements had been the catalyst for their subsequent hook-up; in his words, "Shall I postulate an undying devotion to your lips of flaming octopus?"), I may have paved the way for their future relationship by referencing the commonality of our English majors.

Not that at the time I had felt any tingling at the sight of Ricky's mammoth endowments. In fact, I was originally turned off by her, although there was something pleasing about her face, but she was too loud, too vulgar, and her eyes were framed by thick lenses that gave her the look that she was trying too hard, and too soon, to see into the hidden depths of your being so that she could then, as was her annoying habit, like an Alfred J. Prufrock, "encapsulate you in a phrase." It was only after she had moved into the apartment next to mine on Amsterdam Avenue in the West Side—by which time Ishmael was having an extramarital affair with her (he was married and had a little girl, whom he described as someone he was waiting for to see "the light in the corner of her eye to start paving the way," or the start of her consciousness)—that lascivious thoughts about Ricky started crawling into my mind, like the roaches that dominated the nights in my apartment at the dying of the light.

So I began to see Ricky through the romanticized eyes of the mad poet; his mad passion for her began to seep through the sluices of my own imagination. This passion melt was heated by our walks at night through the sultriest parts of Harlem, when, supposedly, he was looking for the option of death and I was looking for the lightning-laminated words to water the desiccated ground of my impoverished imaginareum, oblivious to the fact that white eyeballs red with rage in black faces turned toward us like weather vanes warning of the storm to come.

The parties that Ricky and I hosted together added to my growing desire to knead with my own hands the doughy flesh that the mad poet had already palmed. When the flammable brew of our parties, fueled by beer and lit by marijuana cigarettes, combusted into free-for-all fights, Ricky would pronounce the party a success on the basis of her observation that no party was a success until the cops had had the last dance. This only deepened my desire to bury my fingers into the glutinous mass of her soft body.

59

Claremont Boys

The old hood had changed overnight. Like the street sweeper sweeping through at dawn and removing in its mechanical broom's vortex the crushed cigarette butts, the rolling plastic soda bottles, the twisted beer cans, the debris of yesterday's life, so had the new immigrants replaced the old: the Blacks replaced the Irish and Italians, the Puerto Ricans the Jews, now ensconced in the brick fortresses of Co-Op City. The old Hebrew National Deli on Claremont Parkway and Washington Avenue had likewise undergone radical change; it had been appropriated by our little gang, our clique of salsa-loving, *pachanga*-dancing, beer-guzzling young Latinos who spent our evenings listening to and jumping up and down to the rhythms of Johnny Pacheco and his *charanga* band.

It was my last year at City College, and in order to finish—as my parents' ability to subsidize my education had reached its breaking point—I had obtained a job in the evening at what was then Manufacturer's Trust Bank, in its stock transfer division. I was hired to work the shift from five p.m. to one a.m., but usually, since we wrapped up at around ten p.m., our supervisor, John, would let us off the hook and send us home. That meant that I would come on the scene off the old Third Avenue El on Claremont Parkway at around eleven. To my heart's joy and my wallet's pain, I would hit the street to the waiting welcome of my home boys. Like a visiting dignitary, I would be mobbed and escorted like a celebrity to the deli, where I would soon be jumping up and down with my homies, everyone holding up a bottle of Schaeffer like a glass partner in their hand, courtesy of Manufacturer's, *pachangando* the night away.

"Hey, Joey," my boy and protective shadow, Big Eddie, would shout above the crowd's din and Pacheco's flute, "how about some . . ." as he made, with his thumb and index finger, the universal sign for smoking weed that indicated that it was time to go cop some, over by Tremont Avenue, where, through a small round hole in a front door in a walk-up porch, we (I) would insert a fiver and *presto*, a small bag of sinsemilla would pop out, as easy as buying M&Ms from a vending machine. Big Eddie would then roll a joint in the dark adjoining alley with his large, meaty fingers, which were as dexterous in rolling a smooth, unwrinkled joint of the quality of a fresh Pall Mall as they were when doubled up into a fist to threaten or smash into the face of some delinquent account of the loan shark at the hospital on whose behalf he collected.

When we got back to the deli after doing the doobie, the whole atmosphere would seem changed: the *charanga* beat cleaner, the light more luminescent, the glow in others' eyes a watt or two higher. After some more *pachangas* and more beering, with the light of the joint still sparkling in the alcohol-sogged cells in my brain, I would make my zig-zaggy way home to our railroad apartment on Third Avenue, where, as if on cue, mami would already have on the stove my late-night dinner of roasted pork chops, rice and beans, and *guineitos maduros*. And then bedtime, with my Hollywood bed popping up and down in my brain in time with the lyrics:

Yo tengo un chivo,
Mantengo y mantengo un chivo,
A mi mujer no le gusta el chivo.

60

Trading Thoughts

It was the heady days of the sixties, of real and hypothetical revolutions, of social and artistic ferment. That old tree of knowledge was sprouting new leaves, bearing new fruits; its seeds would be the plantings of future generations to come. At City College, the gnarled roots of old ideas were being reburnished by men with new intellectual spades.

At the snack bar in Finley Hall, where we all congregated, each little plot of territory was occupied by intellectual flowerings of many different hues and fragrances. In that corner over there, the hammer-and-sickle crowd cultivated ideas of shady revolutions, of a new, equalitarian society that would spring up from the razed stubble of fallen capitalism; across from them, Maoists and their acolytes, the Students for a Democratic Society (SDS), debated the virtues of bringing glass marbles to the confrontation with the NYPD mounted troops in their next planned demonstration; in the garden of the ROTC students, the Vietnam War and talk of falling dominoes were the plantings of the day.

Our corner, the poets' corner, was a conservatory of new poetic and artistic forms. Rooted at its center was our leader, Pablo, a poet of exquisite pentameters and metaphors of triple pruning. Today, he was advancing the theory that, to quote him, "poetry is, per se, the highest art, since in its rhythms it incorporates music, and in its imagery, the whole of visual arts."

Opposite him, Ishmael, the mad poet, held forth a more apocalyptic vision. To him, poetry was the art of the lunatic. He said, "In that madman's fusion of confusion, there's not one hair's breadth of doubt that to change the grey rock red, the moon must first decide to worship the relativity of things."

Between them stood I, balancing myself on their Virgilian words, wondering whether the small seeds of poetry that I carried in my clenched fist would ever find the nurturing ground that would bear the fruits of my longing.

61

West Side Blues

I was suffering from post-graduation depression, similar to post-partum depression: after five and a half years at City College, after much laboring in the pregnant fields of intellectual pursuits, I had given birth to a parchment baccalaureate and I was unhappy, unfulfilled. Smoking pot hadn't helped, and it didn't seem to help my writing, either. Nights I would spend with a joint in one hand and a pen in the other, and in the baleful mornings when I cast a bloodshot eye to view the "masterpiece" that I thought I had created in my semi-hallucinogenic stage, instead of metaphors brimming with Socrates' flare I would discover gibberish that would disintegrate in the dawning light.

It didn't help that I had dumped my girlfriend, Laura, either, and I could no longer lean on that stout pillar of feminine optimism or reflect myself in the mirror of her semi-mythic adulation of me.

The problem was that I now had huge pockets of time at my disposal and no change to fill them with. Gone were the afternoons at the City College cafeteria with my fellow poets, with Pablo, the Pope of Poetry, theorizing how poetry was the highest art since it combined the visual and musical arts with philosophy, to form the mega substance of reality; or with Ishmael, the mad poet, who wanted to climb his "pagoda to its highest peak, and be the keeper of silence"; or at the Ibero-American Club on Tuesday afternoons, where poets and singers and *declamadores* and flamenco dancers would make their startling appearances and leave us with the keen frisson of those who had brushed up against "Art," an excitement much like that of accidentally brushing up against a beautiful woman on a crowded subway in New York City.

Now, all alone in my fifth-floor walk-up on Amsterdam Avenue, with a window that faced the blank brick wall of the building opposite mine, I did bewail my outcast state, sans love, sans coins, sans hope, sans anything.

My mom would come over from time to time, with my stepfather, Joe, who drove her over from the Bronx to bring me some of the elixirs of life—homemade chicken soup, *chuletas, arroz con gandules*—and find me as lifeless as a stray whelp that had been beaten up and abused and left semi-comatose on some curb in the street. She would give me a few spiritual *pases*, intone some incantatory prayers from her spiritual playbook to free those possessed of melancholic spirits, and, seeing how little her powers of *curandera* worked on me, would then shake me and shout, "*Sacudete*, Toño, *sacudete.*" But I could not or would not shake myself; my melancholy was self-imposed, and it would take a season of self-imposed sadness before I could *sacudir* myself, awaken the sad whelp that I had become, bestir myself, shake my coat of fur, waggle my tail, and run out into the world, panting, to meet whatever fate would mete out to me.

Part IX

A MATURE ADULT IN NYC

62

An Encounter with
Eddie of the Second Kind

Eddie and I were *panitas*, meaning that, as the corruption of the English word "partner" implies, we were close buddies in the Claremont Parkway neighborhood of the South Bronx, where we used to hang out and party together. Our party headquarters was a former Jewish deli restaurant on Claremont Parkway and Washington Avenue that, with the exodus of its former Jewish customers to Co-Op City and other places farther north in the Bronx, our Latino crowd had taken over and made into our beer and *pachanga* joint; Eddie loved to drink beer and to dance *la pachanga*, which the rest of us did also, it being the kind of dance that we could do as a group, with each guy doing his thing separately from each other.

Pachanga is a simple dance to describe but difficult to execute, as it involves slipping and sliding on the balls of your feet while maintaining the rhythm of Johnny Pacheco's music, with its flute accompaniment, which is the sine qua non of the *pachanga*. Eddie, as heavy and bulky as he was, was nevertheless a graceful dancer, and his sense of rhythm was heightened by the little smoke we would cop in a house near Tremont Avenue, where, after we put in our order for a "dime" and slipped a folded ten-dollar bill through a small round hole in the door, the baggie of pot would pop out, like getting candy from a vending machine. Pot was our candy, and like candy, when you inhaled that magic smoke, you began immediately to savor life in a sweet and magical way; Pacheco's *flauta* took on the qualities of bird songs in the field, and your feet responded like you were dancing on a cushion of pneumatic air.

Those happy days hanging out on Claremont Parkway gradually faded away, and time, with its giant and inexorable eraser, rubbed away that scene and replaced it with scenes drawn on new canvases. I had gone on to marry, have children, and obtain my master's in social work (MSW) degree from Hunter School of Social Work, and I was now senior counselor at the Melrose Rehabilitation Center, a program to treat narcotic addicts. I was very happy at my job, and worked with an excellent staff, consisting of both professionals and paraprofessionals. The particular mission of the unit was to develop jobs in the community for the recovering addicts. This gave me a lot of satisfaction and brought me into direct contact with some of the power centers in the community, heads of corporations, political clubs, hospital administrators, and other sources of employment and influence.

So, who should break through the misty clouds of my happiness but Eddie, who showed up on my floor one afternoon and greeted me with a look of surprise followed by one of his familiar but powerful bear hugs.

"Joey," he says to me, "it's great to see you. It's been a long time, man."

"Yes, it has, Eddie, a long time," I said.

"I'm so glad to see that you are here, too," he said, making a fist in a salute of solidarity. "Listen, Joey, let's hook together and control this shit, total control, you know, and have these fucking junkies eating out our hands, me and you, you know, like the old *panitas* that we were."

The streets of Claremont Parkway, the deli, the place where we use to cop pot, and the whole *pachanga* scene flashed through my mind at that moment like a film rolling by at warp speed. Then, clearing my throat to swallow away those memories, I said, "Eddie, you don't understand. I am the supervisor."

Eddie's eyes shuttered and stuttered for a second and then, embracing me in a polar bear-like hug this time, he said, "Joey, you're the man, you're the man," and with that, he walked out of the program, never to return again.

63

Virgil and Horace

My two long-lost college friends, both poets, whom I shall call Virgil and Horace, came to revisit me in a dream, a fugue of college past.

Virgil, who, perhaps in sophomoric reaction to the pseudo-intellectualism abounding at CCNY, like that of those who studied and spouted Egyptian hieroglyphics or ancient Minoan mounds, wrote:

"Can you not see, can you not tell, that the intellectual vitamin is not enough?"

And Horace, who wrote the astonishing couplet:

"There never was in you a pound of steam,

You useless radiator of my dream."

My masters, as they were wont to do in our college days, continued to enlighten me on the construction of metaphors:

"Words, by themselves, signify nothing," they intoned. "They are really screens behind which hide the speaker's intent. Metaphors, on the other hand, are double- or triple-edged, like standing at a street corner where you can look down one, two, three, four streets at once rather than one."

64

Ghetto and Shtetel

If it weren't for my wife, I would still be "ghetto," but with my wife, I'm kind of "shtetel." Betwixt the two and the twain, that is, before I met and grated my wife, I were a bona fide, dyed-in-the-wool, wooled-in-the-dye member of the Puerto Rican tribe, that species of folk who strut their stuff in mambo rooms, where the hot, breasty breath of the Latin mamas contain enough sweetness of cannabis to give you a contact high and bathrooms hang close and tight with the acridness of cocaine. Yeah, I were there once, in the hustle, pedaling smoke, smoking the petal in my hip-hop ride, with Mac wheels and the Lone Star flag flapping upside down on the visor, jetting smoke from the gleaming chrome tailpipes like twin octopuses hiding, high-tailing high from *la hara*.

But then I felt her soft, Semitic embrace, and the Mac wheels came off, and the smoke went up in smoke, and the Latin ballrooms were wheeled off the stage, and on to the podium of Carnegie came Bernstein, and onto the stage Beethoven, harrowing the heart with arrows from violin bows, so how could I not go shtetel?

65

The Comanche Kid

(TO BE READ BY PROSPECTIVE FATHERS WHILE WAITING AND EXPECTING)

Sharon's OB/GYN doctor, may he rest in peace—although peace is the only state in which I can imagine him, in a heaven in which reproductive providers are not in much demand due to the strictures up there against marrying and giving in marriage—was the one who was able to convince my wife, Sharon (née Youngerman, née Jewish), that the best course in an interfaith, inter-ethnic, and therefore inter-strife marriage was one of compromise; "compromise" was the exact word he used, a word that, once pronounced, rendered itself as Solomonic, as we could not possibly divide the future human being that frolicked in her belly like an acrobat in a weightless and watery spacecraft, and who once in a while kicked up his heels for sheer joy, into two parts: one, Hispanic Christian, trailing behind him the debris of two millennia of rosaries of religious wars, masses of genocide of native peoples, Inquisitions, auto-da-fé, forced conversions, and all the other wonderful achievements of the Holy Faith; the other, European Jewry, trailing behind him, in a converse fashion, the same dust of Inquisitions, forced conversions, etc. etc., only in their case, in a reverse and perverse experience.

No, he was one human being, this aquatic acrobat, and as such could not be pulled, as though he were a human rubber band, into two opposite directions, for fear of breakage. Not that he was overly eager to come out anyway when the exit lights came on in the intra-belly darkness he was inhabiting with uninhibited joy; the doctor said that, apparently, he had managed to twist himself into an undeliverable position that even a yogi would envy, and besides that, from what I could gather from an attending nurse's under-the-breath comment, Sharon was showing signs of partum weariness.

At some point, the obstetrician came out of the delivery room to advise me that if this situation did not improve by morning, he would have to go in the way Caesar went into Rome, the Cesarean way. In the meantime, I should go home and rest; there was nothing I could do there by the side of the rubicon (a.k.a. the East River) whose bank Doctors' Hospital straddled, overlooked Gracie Mansion, where Mayor Lindsay was, I'm sure, himself on watch, although for entirely different reasons.

Reassured, I drove home to the other shoulder of Manhattan, to our apartment on Riverside Drive, to sleep a few discomfited hours, and returned to the hospital early the next morning, when things, thank god, proceeded as normal. They had managed to uncoil the recalcitrant yogi from his head stance; thereafter, he had slid down the chute of life, like a child down a playground slide, landing happily into this world with such a gleam of intelligence and sensitivity in his fully opened, soulful eyes, that it made Wordsworth's words that we are born "trailing clouds of glory" more than just a metaphor growing amid fields of golden daffodils. Born with a reddish hue to his complexion, as though blessed by an Indian shaman, and a full headdress of untamed dark hair, such that, when I came to view him at the nursery (the name on his bassinette was "Baby Camacho"), the nurse hollered, "Bring out the Comanche Kid."

Part X

AN OLD MAN IN NYC

66

My Life under the Table

Hi! My name is José and I'm an alcoholic and a pothead. I make this confession freely and without coercion, in an attempt at self-healing—which may, to some and sometimes, seem an oxymoron (with the emphasis on moron, bearing in mind the dictum that a lawyer who represents himself has a fool for a client). Nevertheless, this attempt at healing myself through the process of internal therapy on a one-to-none basis is one that I undertake as a means of self-generation in the hope that my training as a social worker and therapist can help me to clarify and deal with the issues of substance abuse that have played a large and destructive part in my life. The tip of the spur that has led me to this examination, like so many of our self-revelations, began with a recent dream that I had.

In this dream, I was driving in a car that was going in reverse on a highway that bordered a green and beautiful mountain, with a more scenic road on a higher plateau parallel to the road I was on. I was driving in reverse because I wanted to reach the entrance ramp of that higher and more scenic road. I kept stepping on the gas and accelerating more and more, and the road that I was on was itself becoming more and more elevated, but I could not find the entrance to the other, higher road. I continued to accelerate and elevate at the same time, until I was ascending to the point where I was higher than the mountain; eventually, I was elevated past the confines of the earth, past the beautiful blue-and-brown globe of the earth that has been captured in some of the photographs from the missions in space, and into sidereal space. I was weightless, floating, in my own silent cocoon of indescribable *goia*. Yet, at the dream's end, in that moment of bliss, I had not achieved my goal; the entrance to that road that I had sought had eluded me, and I awoke, unfulfilled.

Being, as I am, of a Jungian bent of mind, believing, as he did, that dreams contain the seeds of our regeneration, that they offer, in a mandala type of way, a clue to resolving the central dilemmas of our psychic life, it occurred to that my dream was posing the central question of my dilemma while at the same time offering a possible solution. The dream was telling me that at some point in my life I took the wrong road, that there was another road I could have taken, a higher one, more scenic and fulfilling, that would have actualized me more as a person and human being. It also suggested that no matter how hard I tried, driven, to find the entrance to that other road, no amount of back-pedaling could ever return me to that original place where I became separated from my higher self, but that in the process of examining the when, how, and why of that separation I would find joy, the self's ultimate joy, or *goia*.

The "when and the how": under the table.

Drinkers like to boast that they can drink anybody "under the table," that they will still be standing and drinking while their fellow drinking buddies lie in a comatose state under the figurative table. In the cruel paradox of the turn of phrase that I am about to employ, when I began my drinking life at the wee age of five or six, I was already and literally under the table. The table that I was under was in the kitchen of our apartment in the South Bronx, circa 1945–6, where I and my young cohorts were hiding from the rest of the guests celebrating the good fortune of our immigrant family in obtaining jobs and its attendant greenbacks in our new adopted country.

I had been given what, to me, being a sociable and gregarious child, much advanced in manner, dress, and conversation than the years stated on my birth certificate, was the pleasant duty of serving, in these little, tiny glasses a cheap, red, oversweet Manischewitz wine that our esteemed guests politely sipped and just as politely left half consumed. And, of course, it was my sociable, gregarious self, much advanced in manner, dress, and conversation, who was assigned the task of retrieving the glasses with the leftover wine. And then, of course, I was to politely and pleasantly pour the sweet and pleasant-smelling wine down the sink, which, of course, I did not do. Instead, I spirited the spirits away under the table, where I, with my little co-conspirators, proceeded to pour the sweet, intoxicating wine down the drains of our little throats, where, in my case, as the leading conspirator with the biggest drain and draught, the sweet elixir made its way through my internal pipes into the as-yet-not-fully formed labyrinth of my childish brain, producing the *goia* of the primal euphoria.

But, of course, just as a clogged drain will spew out its unwanted load, so did my brain, in chemical overload, strongly command my esophageal drain to constrict and contract, and I spewed the intoxicating elixir, which spread, like an red and angry Rorschach stain, all over the kitchen floor. That was the when and how of my under-the-table life. The "why" is much harder to come by.

Or perhaps not so hard, after all, when you consider the properties of alcohol and its effects on the human body. When, for example, you rub alcohol on your skin, as it evaporates it cools your skin and feels refreshing, relieving whatever itch is bothering you. So on the heart. When it rubs there, it evaporates whatever itch that the gnat of time and fortune may have engendered there, cooling and refreshing it. But alcohol also catches fire easily, as when they ignite the cognac poured on your dessert in a restaurant. So is your heart ignited, and it can dance and sing with fires of joy and whisper of endless possibilities. Once singed by that swich liquor, singing and dancing by the fire of joy, stepping away from the flames into the darkness of your own personal cave becomes a Sisyphean task: you haul the rock of your willpower up to the crest of your sobriety only to see it roll back on the next occasion when the fire catches again, for its embers have never totally gone out, and the thirst for its joy has never really slackened completely, away.

Thus, a shy, acne-plagued teenager becomes a dashing Lothario under the influence, and the cowardly lion begins to roar with false self-confidence, and soon, repressed impulses pulse to the fore and you enter the chamber of endless possibilities. But the chamber is really nothing but a bubble, bursting upon you with piercing headaches, a dry throat, and desiccated dreams.

This you know, with the knowledge of a thousand wasted nights, with the mirages of hundreds of potent-less conquests, and yet, you come back, as though the promise of breaking on through is more than lyrics from the Doors song. But wait, there is a point in which getting high brings you to a plane higher on the brain, where insight tears through the Maya of every day's quota of humdrumness and emotions, long lukewarming in the cup of ordinary being, to bubble and rise again with newfound taste. Music acquires new contrasts, notes glisten with new sensuality, metaphors stand on street corners with vistas of streets not noticed before, and life envelops you with unfamiliar kisses and embraces.

Your own dear ones, your beloveds, shed their time-worn and wrinkled garments of raveled familiarity and are born again to the newfound love your re-enlightened vision shines on their memory.

This ode to life takes on a newer mode
And olden songs by molten fires sing
Re-visioned visions revive old hymns
And life relived revives the spirit's spring.

67

The Hudson Valley Writers' Center — A Satire in the Key of F

It was the third Friday of the month, and the clock was fast approaching seven thirty, the bewitching hour when the writers and the poets and the comedians and new and old essayists would strut and fret their five minutes on the stage (some of them from whom you would hear no more).

While the cookies were laid out on the table and the coffee was steaming hot with aromatic scent, there was something missing: usually, at this hour, the Hudson Valley Writers' Center would be teeming with folks rustling papers containing their new, if unacknowledged, masterpieces, biting their lips in nervous anticipation of going on stage, or, in the case of some of our male writers, scanning the place to see if there were any new and interesting female writers in the crowd with whom to share a paragraph or two; tonight, the seats were all empty, except for José, who, like a perennial flower, was always present and blooming with new stories about Caguas or the South Bronx or the Puerto Rican migration, and Sharon, his wife, his perennial companion, who also bloomed with smiles of encouragement and good things to say to all the writer-readers, from her kind and sweet soul that viewed the world through the prism of confectionery lenses.

Ryan, the director of the Center, was frantic with worry. He turned to the host of that night, Pat, and asked her, "What are we going to do? We have only José to read, and you know, he always times his piece to five minutes on the dot" (after multiple rehearsals at home under the watchful eye of sweet Sharon, with a stop watch in her hand to mark the time). Pat said, "Well, see what José has; tell him he can read as much of his material as he has, no time limit this time."

"This is all you have?" Pat asked José, "This page and half of writing, with only a measly four hundred and fifty words, or twelve point eight kilo bites? This will take you less than five minutes!"

"No," José said, with the gestures and the accent and the bells and whistles that come at the end, "it's exactly five minutes, right, Sharon?" Sharon dutifully held up her stop watch and sweetly nodded in agreement.

"Well," Pat complained to José, "why didn't you bring more stuff? You see the bind we're in?"

José answered, "How would I have known? You're usually hung up on this time thing, and some of the hosts even bring in an egg timer that goes off with this terrible sound that makes you want to rush to some oven to take the scorched cake out, and it ruins my ending, which is usually the best part of my stories, or you have someone with a Blackberry ready to twitter to all of his friends on Facebook how I trespassed the time limit again, or someone who pushes you off the stage or turns the mike off or turns the lights out, or whatever, isn't that right, Sharon?" who nodded again from the audience with a sweet smile.

"What are we going to do?" Pat asked Ryan. "José has only five minutes exactly of writing, and he is stubbornly sticking to it with his wife's backing. She's seated over there waving that stupid stop watch in the air."

"Well," Ryan said, "tell him to read it slowly, say one word every five minutes, until the whole two hours are used up."

But José had a better idea. Why not read his story in many languages?

"Bon jour messieurs, j'ai cette nuit une conte apelle the Hudson Valley Writers' Center . . ."

"Buenos dias, senores, tengo aqui un cuento titulado . . ."

And so it went all night, from Spanish to French, to Tagalog to Swahili, to the obscure clicking languages of the sub-Sahara and even pig Latin, which José had picked up on the streets of the South Bronx, and *cha chi cha chi cha cha*, the pig Latin of school children in Puerto Rico, until the two hours expired and everyone went home: the director, Pat, José with his script, and sweet Sharon, waving her stop watch in triumph.

68

The Corridors of Memory

Every time, it seems, that I peer into the mirror of my prose or stumble down the corridors of my dreams, I am met with the image of my stepfather, Joe, who, although deceased, haunts those corridors and mirrors like after-flashes of a life that will not fade. For someone like me, raised in the ambiance of spiritualists and faith healers and worshippers of Baba-lu and the Seven African Potentates, there is a spookiness in these dreams, for, although in them Joe is smiling and seems gracious enough, he also seems to be beckoning me to follow him, ostensibly to some happy place, like a picnic or a beach, but that, I fear, may be beyond the line where re-entry to this world would not be allowed.

Like into the wastebasket of discarded crumpled pieces of scribbles, I reach in to recover memories of times we spent in each other's company (not always happy ones), something stiff and informal that always seemed to infuse our interactions, like strangers who were always meeting.

69

The Dybbuk

Imagine that there is life after death. Imagine that after you have shed that threadbare but cherished garment of flesh, your spirit still haunts your old familiar places, like your body odor lingering in your walk-in closet, while the powers above mull the decision to either pull you up to celestial glory or sink you down to that place where your sins are lined up like pictures on a wall. And while you are waiting for that elevator, with an anxious eye as to whether the green button for up will appear or the dreaded red button for down, you have a little time down here to settle some scores with some of the people who did you or are even now doing your memory wrong.

Imagine. Because you haven't yet been cleansed of evil thoughts. You still cling to them like a child to its doll. Let's see; which doll are you going to sink a needle into? Your dybbuk eyes naturally settle on the one person who was, in all his goyim ways, the most virulent antagonist to your orthodoxy: your brother-in-law, who even now is cleansing your memory from your apartment. Those treasured souvenirs from the blessed land? Out to the Salvation Army! Your sacred books and holy objects? Out, out. All your memories being swiped away with a smutty Gentile cloth!

In anger, the dybbuk soul now expands to golem proportions: revenge in life is sweet, but revenge after life is sweeter—and silent, the shrouded silence of the dead. Knowing that this goyim's lips are forever seeking kisses from the lips of bottles, you lead him gently into that good night of the closet, and help him find the liquor bottles that you hid in there, like a trap hidden from an unsuspecting animal. Nudge his elbow to flex your very expensive bottle of cognac to his unclean lips. *Drink mightily at my expense, you benighted fool.*

Now he is running down the stairs of my apartment—my apartment, see—and stumbles on his drunken feet, with a little push from me (wow, I can actually affect material matter on my own with a high degree of concentration, but it drains some of my spiritual reservoir of energy), and there he goes, falling down the stairs headlong onto the hall's cement wall (*ouch*; I myself felt that headbutt!). But my aim was a little off, and he hit the wall with his left temple and didn't concuss his brain (pity), but I still have time left in my roaming and energy left for a few more attempts to even up the score (goyim one, dybbuk zero).

Imagine again that a tiny beam of light, laser-like, has landed on the shoulders of the fallen man. It soon begins to expand like light from a projector when it hits the screen, and a figure appears, draped in a white *Santeria* dress, a dark face hidden under its hood. The figure extends its light onto the fallen man, and the light itself courses through the man's veins, and he comes back to consciousness, with the sense that the light coursing through him is the spirit of his aunt Candida, his guardian angel, who in life loved him and in death protects him.

As the man rises from the floor with the angel's help, the dybbuk retreats into the dark recesses of the landing above, but now he begins to feel that a powerful force, like a giant magnet, is pulling him away. It pulls him through the wall, beyond the earth's own pull, beyond the galaxies that rush past him like swirls of snowflakes. He is whirling in outer space, not knowing what direction he's going—up or down or sideways—for in that space beyond space there is no up or down, there is no today or tomorrow nor memory of revenge or hope, but only the dissolution of his mass as it is blown away by a giant breath into the black hole of eternity.

70

Trading Worlds

Sometimes, as if in a dream, I feel the tug and pull of my deceased mother calling me from the other world, and sometimes my stepfather joins her, calling me, pulling me into their dimension of nonexistence. Come, come, they seem to say, it's not so bad out here; we miss you.

It's as though their relationship to me has been inverted; when they were on this side of the border that now and forever separates us, they urged care upon me. Don't drive too fast, don't smoke too much, don't get into fights. Now they urge: jump off the ledge, drink, drink, drink, smoke, smoke, smoke.

O, Epicurus and Lucretus, I wish I shared your equanimity in the face of death! I wish I could myself believe the philosophy I espouse to my friends, when they quote Hamlet, that that undiscovered country from whose bourn no man returns puzzles the will. It's no puzzle, I tell them with disguised non-confidence; it's really very simple. Where were you before you were born? For billions and billions of years before you were born, you were dead. You didn't exist. And for billions years more you will also not exist. Death is something you are very familiar with, as your nonexistence preceded you and will succeed you. You live within mirror images of eternity.

I wish it were that simple and that I had the courage of my non-convictions.

But at my back I always hear that winged chariot drawing near, and as the shades beckon me, I suddenly recover my will to live and urge the shades away; yet as the shadows retreat, their non-solidarity melting away before the light of my regained enthusiasm to remain in this world, I sometimes cry out, Wait, wait for me, don't go! I love you, too, I miss you.

Untitled

Death, which loves to undress us of our flesh,
Cannot undress the memory I have of you:
How gracefully you shook life's hand
And with the other soothed a child's pain.
No, these remembrances will not be smothered
By that moldering soil that envelops your remains,
But live alongside that picture I have of you, smiling.
Yo, death, you'll have no victory as long as memory clothes my heart.

José A Camacho
undated

Postcard of Caguas

Jose's grandparents with his cousin in front of their house in Caguas, PR.

*Jose's grandmother with his cousin and chickens
in the backyard of the house in Caguas, PR.*

*Jose's birthday cake picture at a photo studio
in the Bronx, as described in a story.*

Jose with his mother and brother on a rooftop in the Bronx, NY.

The front of the family house in Caguas years after the family all left.

About the Author

This collection of short stories of Jose Camacho's life in Puerto Rico and New York City reflects his lifelong love of writing as well as his appreciation for his bicultural upbringing. His wit, charm, and passion for language shine through each of these windows into his unique life experiences.

Jose was born in Caguas, Puerto Rico, in 1940, and moved to the Bronx with his family in 1945. He graduated from City College of New York with a degree in English and a minor in Spanish, and later earned an MSW (master of social work). Jose used his skills and humanity to make a difference in the lives of the populations he served; he was a caseworker for the New York City Department of Social Services, a counselor for the New York State Drug Abuse Control Commission, and a counselor at two New York State correctional facilities.

Jose was married for more than fifty years to his beloved wife, Sharon, with whom he raised two sons in Westchester County, New York. He was proud of their personal and professional successes, and had the pleasure of watching his two grandchildren grow and achieve academic and creative achievements. Jose died of complications from COVID in February 2021.

www.ingramcontent.com/pod-product-compliance
Lightning Source LLC
Chambersburg PA
CBHW061521120726
48001CB00004B/1382